The Ultimate Guide
TO VEGETABLE SIDE DISHES

Rebecca Lindamood

Author of *Not Your Mama's Canning Book* and *Ready, Set, Dough!*

PAGE STREET
PUBLISHING CO.

PAGE STREET
PUBLISHING CO.

First published in 2020 by

Page Street Publishing Co.

27 Congress Street, Suite 105

Salem, MA 01970

www.pagestreetpublishing.com

Distributed by Macmillan, sales in Canada by The Canadian Manda Group.

24   23   22   21   20   1   2   3   4   5

ISBN-13: 978-1-64567-085-8

ISBN-10: 1-64567-085-6

Library of Congress Control Number: 2019957247

Cover and book design by Laura Benton for Page Street Publishing Co.

Photography by Rebecca Lindamood

Printed and bound in China

Page Street Publishing protects our planet by donating to nonprofits like The Trustees, which focuses on local land conservation.

Dedication

Contents

Introduction

. . . .

Have you ever stood looking at a vegetable that you bought, that was given to you by a gardener friend, or that you received in a CSA share, blanked out, and thought, "Well what am I supposed to do with this?" I think we've all been there. It's hard enough to get a main dish on the table most nights, let alone think of a side dish that goes with it.

The Ultimate Guide to Vegetable Side Dishes is the solution to that common conundrum; the delicious answer to how to use up all the produce that you have handy.

This book is my love letter to vegetables. Recipes are conveniently organized into mini chapters for each type of vegetable and each and every one has a recommendation for the type(s) of main dish(es) it accompanies best. Each chapter begins with indispensable information on choosing the best of that vegetable and storage tips on how long to store them. There's even a helpful section called Side Dish Improvers (page 245)—delicious infused oils, sauces, or dressings that make vegetable side dishes so good that they'll tempt even picky eaters.

That's not all you'll get out of these pages, though I love these recipes madly. From what to look for at the grocery store/produce stand to the ideal way to store potatoes and onions (hint: not together!) I have you covered. Every recipe in this book is designed to use vegetables that you'll find in most farmers markets, CSA shares, and grocery stores in North America and Europe.

And if you're trying to feed picky eaters, I am here to tell you there's hope.

Meals should be one of life's great pleasures, not a power struggle of epic proportions. I cannot guarantee this will be the holy grail to help you with all picky eaters in your life, but I can promise you this; I love each and every recipe in this book, and the great majority of them were deemed "tasty" by even the now older, more open-minded, formerly anti-veg contingent.

It helped that we used highly flavorful recipes and made sure we cooked the vegetables in ways that optimized their texture and natural flavors. The happy result of those years of experiments and my experience in getting kids to try different things are both in this book.

I'll share my strategies with you in the No, Thank You Very Much chapter on page 10. I hope that my time in the trenches can help give hope to a parent or guardian out there who's ready to throw up the white flag and surrender to a lifetime of hot dogs and boxed mac and cheese requests.

Rebecca Lindamood

Vegetables for Days

WHERE TO FIND THE BEST PRODUCE IF YOU DON'T HAVE A GREEN THUMB.

If you have a beautiful vegetable garden, I bow to you. Each attempt at gardening has proven to me that I lack the talent or patience to grow vegetables prolifically. I am pretty good at growing pickling cucumbers and zucchini, harvesting a few tomatoes, and keeping herbs alive, but that's about it.

I am, however, excellent at shopping for, sourcing, and storing the tastiest vegetables, though. This is good because I love vegetables and can't grow them reliably to save my life.

WHERE TO FIND THE BEST PRODUCE

While I am fortunate to have some extremely talented gardeners amongst my family and friends, I can't count on them for all of my vegetable needs because that would be lazy and selfish, so I have become good at sourcing vegetables. Outside of the kindness of my gardening loved ones' hearts, I have five main ways that I procure vegetables and none of them involves theft.

FARM STANDS

Roadside farm stands are my all-time favorite way to get great bargains on vegetables. Farm stands are plentiful during the growing season, even though it's short in duration where I live and they are a great way to grab dinner-sized amounts of tomatoes, potatoes, asparagus, winter squash, summer squash or zucchini, and more.

Bonus Tip: If you go frequently and you're friendly with your farmer or gardener, they'll get to know what you like and may be willing to set things aside for you! This is invaluable if you like to can or preserve vegetables or have very specific tastes.

FARMERS' MARKETS

Farmers' markets are as fleeting as farm stands in my part of the world, but they're a great place to procure larger amounts of vegetables and fruits for preservation. The bonus tip for farm stands applies here, too. If you frequent the market and you chat up the vendors, they're likely to be able to help you get the things you're looking for more often!

SUPERMARKETS OR GROCERY STORES

While this may seem obvious, there's more to know than the fact that they sell produce. Grocery stores, by necessity, get produce in that's intended to be sturdy. The produce there is generally cosmetically perfect or close to it and is purchased with an eye to longevity to reduce waste of vegetables that go un-purchased before going bad. What this means is that while it will hold up longer on the shelves, you may end up getting a less-fresh product than if you'd purchased at a farm stand, farmers' market, CSA, or picked it from your own garden.

I purchase staples at the grocery store year round and other produce when my farmers' markets, CSA shares, and vegetable subscription boxes do not provide them.

CSA SHARES

If you haven't heard of CSA shares, let me give you a quick break down. CSA stands for Community Supported Agriculture and what that boils down to is local farmers growing and selling produce in your area. Shares work in a few ways, but the basic idea is that you pay x number of dollars to the farmer at the beginning of the season (so they can buy seeds, hire help, etc. . . .) and you're given x amount of produce each week as it is harvested by the farmer.

CSA shares are an amazing way to get ridiculously fresh food grown by people in your area, thereby supporting your local economy. They're also a great way to introduce yourself to new produce, understand what grows in your area, and challenge yourself to think creatively. I never want to waste the vegetables a neighbor worked so hard to grow, so I think a little harder about how to use them before they go bad!

VEGETABLE SUBSCRIPTION BOXES

Indulge me in a little fangirl moment, would you? I love vegetable subscription boxes. They're a relatively new player in the produce market, but they're amazing. In a nutshell, you pay a certain amount of money and you're sent a box full of perfectly delicious and fresh produce. Why?

Well, the models differ slightly, but in the case of one well-known, East Coast vegetable subscription service, they're selling produce that falls just slightly short of the cosmetic requirements of many grocery chains. It's either too big, too small, has some visual blemishes that don't affect the taste or freshness (think three legged carrots, for example), needs a few days on the counter to ripen, or the farmer grew too much to sell all of it . . . but the veggies are fresh, delicious, and wonderful.

Vegetable subscription boxes often sell for a fraction of the cost of the equivalent amount of produce at the store. The catch is that you don't really know what's coming, so it requires you to think fast and have a resource (like this book, lucky you!) to know what to do with it. I've included the names of several of these subscription boxes in the Resources section (page 260) in the back of the book. They're generally limited to certain geographic areas but do sign up to be notified if they expand into your area if they're not already there. And ask your friends if anyone is already subscribing; they may have a discount code for you to use.

HOW TO STORE PRODUCE

One universal rule for storing vegetables for the longest time possible is that you should not wash them until you are ready to use them. I know a lot of kitchen short-cut gurus recommend washing and prepping your food as soon as you get it home from the market, but this accelerates the rate at which vegetables deteriorate in storage. Only do this if you have a solid, bullet-proof meal plan and know you'll use the vegetables according to schedule.

Different vegetables have different benchmarks for freshness and storage tricks. To help keep your crisper drawer fresh and filled, I have compiled a comprehensive guide for you on just what characteristics to look for in each of the vegetables included in this book and how to store those vegetables when you get home. You'll find the information specific to each type of vegetable at the beginning of every chapter.

Important Note: Ethylene is a gas released by certain produce that can cause other produce to ripen faster. For the vegetables described as being ethylene sensitive such as broccoli, cauliflower, eggplants, cucumbers, mushrooms, carrots, and green beans, store them away from apples, apricots, ripe avocados and bananas, figs, kiwis, mangoes, peaches, pears, plums, plantains, tomatoes, and melons.

No, Thank You Very Much:

A STORY OF LIFE WITH PICKY EATERS; AND SOME HOPE

I never gave a lot of thought to vegetables until I had five kids. I mean, outside of a deep enjoyment of eating them, there wasn't much to think about. I didn't just like vegetables, I loved them. I even spent seven young years as a vegetarian.

As a young parent, I had two sons who would eat anything I put in front of them. I had this on lockdown . . . or so I thought. Then I had three sons who were steadfast and united in their dislike of almost all vegetables. There were a few notable standouts: potatoes made the cut for all three of the guys, and the most adventurous of the rest of them welcomed peas, corn, and the occasional carrot onto his plate.

I tried everything I could think of to get them to eat vegetables, with varying degrees of success, but my efforts often met with the kids' favorite response, "No, thank you very much!" in angelic tones.

My first approach was to take the "wait them out" tack. I sat at my plate and ate everything while they sat at their plate and watched me. I informed them they couldn't leave until they at least tried the food. I vastly underestimated the staying power of a child who was dead set against trying something. It was like trench warfare; I hunkered down and hoped they would eat while they hunkered down and hoped I would fall asleep or forget. We were at that table for hours.

After a few rounds of that, I realized it was clearly an ineffective method for us. We needed to get creative.

Being typical young men, I knew my boys were fond of gross stories, so I convinced them to try beets and asparagus by telling them about their effects on bodily functions. It worked short term, but this obviously was not a sustainable way to get them to eat different vegetables on a daily basis; I couldn't very well go on describing the potential effects of all vegetables on their gastrointestinal systems. I got experimental in my bid to get past their formidable defenses.

A friend mentioned to me that large amounts of cheese and butter seemed to be the keys to vegetable bliss at her family's table, and so we tried that next. It worked—hoorah—on some vegetables (think broccoli and cauliflower) but again, this was not a universal solution.

The key to our success turned out to be something that should have been obvious from the start. My husband and I changed our approach from "Please just eat a bite!" and decided to appeal to their senses of adventure. I told stories about the origins of the food, why I loved this or that particular dish so much, where I had learned to make this food, and more.

I talked about how originally, some people had been afraid to eat potatoes and how silly that had all ended up being because everyone knows now that potatoes are delicious. Or how cultivated mushrooms are perfectly safe, but there are very deadly mushrooms found in the wild and asked whether they felt like showing they were tougher than mushrooms.

I made spicy dishes and challenged them to see just how spicy they could handle their food. We changed our attitudes to change theirs.

And most of all, we instituted and respected the one-bite rule as assiduously as we asked for them to respect it. All I asked of them was for them to keep an open mind while trying one bite of each new dish—what we called a "Thank you" bite—and think about it. If they really didn't enjoy it, I didn't force them to eat more or heave deep sighs of disappointment. I'd say, "Maybe someday!" and then my husband and I would polish it off while they tucked into something else at the table they liked more.

. . . But more than once, and with increasing frequency, they went back for a couple of bites just to confirm they didn't like it or—glory, hallelujah—because they decided that they did indeed like the new dish.

So, before we jump into the delicious vegetable-packed side dishes designed to tempt everyone, let me summarize my picky eater approach in four easy-to-remember rules:

1. No battlefields at the table.

2. Keep presenting vegetables and showing that you enjoy them yourself.

3. Make it an adventure. Learn about the foods and talk about them.

4. Keep the "Thank you" bite rule going both ways. If they take one bite with an open mind, don't force anymore and thank them for trying.

POTATOES

By the logic shared by Brillat-Savarin when he said, "Tell me what you eat and I will tell you what you are," I am a potato.

Even in the pickiest days of my kids' picky eating phases, potatoes were one thing they all loved. My repertoire of potato recipes is accordingly vast and I'm sharing my best with you here.

Put down the milk and pick up the cream cheese for Magic 3-Ingredient Mashed Potatoes (page 14), the last mashed potato recipe you'll ever need. Take a culinary trip to western New York for our iconic and amazing Fireman's Chicken Barbecue Salt Potatoes (page 17) and our Buffalo wing–inspired Buffalo-Roasted Potatoes (page 18).

You may have had baked potatoes but unless you've made them with this method, you haven't tasted how sublime a baked potato can be. Thankfully, The World's Best (and Easiest!) Baked Potatoes recipe (page 21) is as easy as can be!

SHOPPING TIPS: Look for clean, firm potatoes with a smooth skin and no cuts, bruises, or discoloration. If you find you have potatoes with green areas or green skin, cut the green areas away before cooking as they can be bitter and unpleasant. If you have potatoes with sprouts, cut the sprouted part away before cooking and eating. There are many varieties of potatoes out there from waxy red, white, purple, or gold potatoes to starchy Russets a.k.a. baking potatoes. These rules apply to all of the varieties of potato.

STORAGE: Contrary to popular practice, storing potatoes under the sink is a bad idea. This is because you want to avoid frequent changes in temperature, and the pipes that carry hot water change temperature frequently. The best bet is a cool (about 43 to 50°F [6 to 10°C]), well-ventilated, dark place (a basement or root cellar) in a perforated plastic bag or in a paper bag. Depending on the freshness of the potatoes, they can keep up to 2 months if stored this way. Count on closer to 1 to 2 weeks at normal room temperature.

Do not be tempted to refrigerate potatoes, as refrigeration converts the starch in potatoes to sugar, which causes an odd, sweet taste and discoloration.

MAGIC 3-INGREDIENT
Mashed Potatoes

Whether you love your mashed potatoes silky smooth or rustic homestyle, with peels or without, or anywhere in between, I'm about to make your mashed potato–lovin' heart very happy. This recipe yields the best mashed potatoes you'll ever eat and it only requires 3 ingredients; yellow potatoes, cream cheese, and butter. Okay, technically you also need the water, but still; these potatoes will thrill you!

YIELD: 10 SERVINGS

INGREDIENTS

5 lbs (2.3 kg) Yukon gold potatoes, peeled (if desired) and quartered

3 tbsp (54 g) kosher salt for the water

1 lb (454 g) butter, softened to room temperature, cut into 1 tbsp (14 g) pats

8 oz (226 g) cream cheese, softened to room temperature

Place the potatoes in a large stockpot. Cover the potatoes by 1 to 2 inches (3 to 5 cm) of water and place the stockpot over high heat. When the water is at a full, rolling boil, add the salt, boil for 15 minutes, or until your potatoes are very tender. You should be able to break them apart easily with the side of a spoon. Use a slotted spoon to transfer the potatoes into a heat-proof bowl. Place the pats of butter and cream cheese in another mixing bowl.

FOR SILKY SMOOTH MASHED POTATOES

Pass the potatoes through a potato ricer or food mill with a medium disc into the bowl with the butter and cream cheese. Stir vigorously with a sturdy spoon until smooth.

FOR RUSTIC HOMESTYLE MASHED POTATOES

Add the drained potatoes to the bowl with the butter and cream cheese and use a hand masher to mash the potatoes to your desired texture. Stir well to incorporate the butter.

NOTE

Because these are so wonderful, they don't need anything else, but add-ins are sometimes fun! Try these great combinations:

Garlic Mashed Potatoes: Add 5 peeled cloves of garlic to the water when you boil the potatoes and mash the cooked cloves into the potatoes.

Bacon-Cheddar-Horseradish Mashed Potatoes: Stir 1 cup each of shredded Cheddar cheese (113 g) and crispy bacon bits (112 g), and ¼ cup (67 g) of prepared horseradish to the mashed potatoes.

Caramelized Onion Mashed Potatoes: Stir in 1 cup (195 g) of caramelized onions (page 227) to the mashed potatoes.

Kitchen Sink Mashed Potatoes: Stir in 2 cups (242 g) of leftover roasted or sautéed vegetables like Spicy Asian Roasted Broccoli (page 32) or Oven-"Seared" Mushrooms (page 142).

FIREMAN'S CHICKEN BARBECUE
Salt Potatoes

If you've had the good fortune to be in the New York countryside on a summer weekend, there's a good chance you've been near a fire department barbecue fundraiser. You'd also know that these potatoes are as ubiquitous to their irresistible grilled chicken meals as hot dogs and burgers are to the rest of the USA in the summer. Fireman's Chicken Barbecue Salt Potatoes are far more exciting (and far less salty tasting) than they sound. Whether you choose to douse them or dunk them in melted butter is up to you, but you'll make these on repeat all year long!

YIELD: 12 SERVINGS

INGREDIENTS

Approximately 3 qts (3 L) water

1¼ cups (365 g) table salt (see Note)

4½ lbs (2 kg) bite-size potatoes, washed and trimmed of any soft or dark spots

1 stick of butter (4-oz [113-g]), melted

Chopped chives, green onions, or parsley to garnish, optional but tasty

SERVE WITH

Grilled or roasted chicken, fish, pork, beef, mushrooms, pot roast, or other braised beef recipes

Bring the water to a boil in a large soup pot or stockpot over high heat. When the water is fully boiling, add the salt and stir to dissolve. When the water returns to a boil, carefully add the potatoes. Do not cover the pan.

Boil for about 20 minutes, or until a knife or fork easily penetrates to the center of the potato when you insert it. Drain the potatoes in a colander and let them air-dry to form the characteristic dry crust.

You can either drizzle melted butter over the potatoes or serve melted butter in a dish at the table for dunking. We are dunkers in our home. Garnish with chives, green onions, or parsley, if desired.

NOTE

It's true that this calls for a crazy amount of salt in the water you use to boil the potatoes. Don't be tempted to reduce the salt, though, as very little of it ends up in the actual potatoes, and it's crucial to the final product. The large amount of salt in the water raises the boiling temperature, making science your partner in creating the creamiest, most perfect boiled potato you'll ever nibble.

BUFFALO-*Roasted Potatoes*

Crispy, mahogany roasted potatoes are the perfect candidate for a quick toss with Garlic Buffalo Wing Sauce (page 55), whether homemade or purchased, and a generous handful each of sliced green onions and minced fresh parsley. For three of my five sons, this is their favorite recipe from this book. Serve these potatoes with grilled, roasted, or fried chicken (obviously!) but they are also great with burgers and hot dogs.

YIELD: 4 SERVINGS

. . . .

INGREDIENTS

4 Russet potatoes, peeled (if desired), cut into roughly 2–3-inch (5–8-cm) pieces (see Notes)

1 tbsp (18 g) kosher salt

¼ cup (60 ml) Luke's Infused Garlic Oil (page 246) or regular olive oil, divided

2–3 tbsp (30–40 ml) Garlic Buffalo Wing Sauce (page 255) or store-bought wing sauce

3 green onions, thinly sliced

3 tbsp (6 g) minced fresh parsley

Preheat the oven to 450°F (232°C). Line a baking sheet with heavy-duty foil, dull side up, and set aside.

Place the potatoes in a pot with the salt, cover with water by 1 inch (2.5 cm), and bring to a boil over high heat. Boil until the potatoes are fork tender, about 10 minutes. Pour the potatoes into a colander and let them air dry for 2 minutes or so, then bang them around a bit by shaking the colander. You want the edges to be a bit rough looking.

Dump the potatoes into a pile on the prepared baking sheet. Drizzle 2 tablespoons (30 ml) of the oil over the potatoes and toss to coat them. Spread them out on the pan, trying to leave a little space between the potatoes.

Roast the potatoes in the preheated oven for 20 minutes, shake the pan, drizzle with the remaining oil, shake again, and roast for another 20 to 25 minutes, or until the potatoes are crisp-edged and deeply golden brown. Transfer the potatoes to a heat-proof bowl and toss with the Garlic Buffalo Wing Sauce, green onions, and parsley. Serve hot, warm, or at room temperature.

NOTES

You can make these using 5 cups (1.6 kg) of leftover Fireman's Chicken Barbecue Salt Potatoes (page 17) that have been halved for a slightly different but equally delicious texture. Simply skip the boiling, but reheat until tender and bang 'em around a bit to soften up the edges.

Even without the wing sauce, these roasted potatoes are pretty spectacular! Feel free to change it up from time to time to try them sauceless.

THE WORLD'S BEST (AND EASIEST!)
Baked Potatoes

As I mentioned in the chapter header, if you are what you eat, then I am in large part potato. My family runs on potatoes, and this is one of our collective favorite ways to have them when the weather is a little chilly. The skins on these potatoes bake up crispy and slightly salty, courtesy of a careful drying and rub down with oil and kosher salt. Don't skip these steps, they're crucial! You can serve these deep brown, crispy skinned beauties with grilled or roasted pork, turkey, chicken, beef or venison, stews or soups, hearty salads, or topped with taco toppings. The sky is the limit!

YIELD: 8 SERVINGS

INGREDIENTS

8 Russet potatoes, washed and thoroughly dried

2 tbsp (30 ml) grapeseed, canola, vegetable, or peanut oil

1 tsp kosher salt

1 tsp ground black pepper

Butter, sour cream, and chopped chives or green onions, optional for serving

Preheat the oven to 425°F (220°C). Rub the potatoes thoroughly with the oil, then with the salt and pepper. Using a fork, poke each potato at least 8 times all over it. Be certain the fork penetrates at least ⅛ inch (3 mm) into the potato each time.

Place the potatoes directly on the preheated oven racks and bake for 40 to 50 minutes, or until the potatoes yield slightly when gently squeezed or reach an internal temperature of 205°F (96°C) when checked with an instant read thermometer.

Jab an "x" into the top of the potatoes with a fork, and press down at the four corners to burst the potatoes open.

If desired, serve with butter, sour cream, and chopped chives or green onions for a beautiful baked potato!

KOREAN SMASHED *Potatoes*

These crispy-edged, creamy-centered, perfectly roasted potatoes are topped with an umami-packed, brick red, slightly spicy, soy sauce–redolent ssamjang sauce that'll be so good you'll want to sing at the top of your lungs. Serve these potatoes with grilled or pan-fried steaks, Korean barbecue pork or beef, or fried chicken.

YIELD: 8 SERVINGS

. . . .

INGREDIENTS

1½ lbs (680 g) baby potatoes or 14–16 leftover Fireman's Chicken Barbecue Salt Potatoes (page 17)

2 tbsp plus ¾ tsp (40 g) kosher salt, divided

½ tsp coarsely ground black pepper

3 tbsp (45 ml) ssamjang sauce (see Note)

2 tbsp (30 ml) toasted sesame oil

1 tbsp (15 ml) rice vinegar

3 tbsp (45 ml) Luke's Infused Garlic Oil (page 246) or olive oil, divided

4 green onions, roots trimmed, thinly sliced

1 tsp toasted sesame seeds

Preheat the oven to 500°F (260°C).

Place the potatoes and 2 tablespoons (36 g) of salt in a large saucepan or small stockpot. Cover the potatoes with water by 1 inch (2.5 cm). Place over high heat and bring to a boil. Reduce the heat and simmer for 20 to 25 minutes, or until the potatoes are tender and easily pierced by a sharp knife or fork. Drain the potatoes in a colander and cool until they're easy to handle but still warm.

Whisk together the ssamjang sauce, sesame oil, and vinegar. Set aside.

Drizzle a rimmed half-sheet pan with 2 tablespoons (30 ml) of the garlic oil. Arrange the potatoes with 2 inches (5 cm) between them. Use a measuring cup to smash each potato lightly, pressing down to break it up and flatten it to about ¾ inch (2 cm) thick. Drizzle the remaining oil over the potatoes then sprinkle with the remaining ¾ teaspoon of salt and the pepper. Roast the potatoes for 20 to 25 minutes, rotating the pan front to back halfway through the cooking time, or until the tops of the potatoes are brown and crispy.

Transfer the potatoes to a serving dish. Use a spoon to drizzle a little of the ssamjang over each potato. Garnish with the thinly sliced green onions and toasted sesame seeds.

NOTE

Ssamjang is available at most Asian grocery stores and many online retailers, but if you can't find it you can make your own. Whisk together ¼ cup (40 g) of Korean soybean paste (doenjang), 2 tablespoons (44 g) of Korean chili paste (gochujang), 2 tablespoons (30 ml) of rice vinegar, 1 tablespoon (15 ml) of honey, 2 teaspoons (6 g) of toasted sesame seeds, and 2 thinly-sliced green onions. Store it in a tightly covered jar in the refrigerator for up to 4 weeks.

CRUNCHY *Potato Wedges* WITH BURGER SAUCE

Your hamburgers and hot dogs have never had a better companion than these cracklingly crunchy, yet fluffy baked potato wedges that are crusted with a buttery Parmesan crust. Don't stop there, though. They're also a fabulous pairing for a pot of chili or soup.

YIELD: 4 SERVINGS

FOR THE POTATO WEDGES

⅓ cup (41 g) all-purpose flour

⅓ cup (33 g) freshly grated Parmesan cheese (Asiago or Romano cheese also work well)

1 tsp smoked paprika

1 tsp kosher salt

⅓ cup (80 ml) milk

3 large Russet potatoes, scrubbed and cut lengthwise into 8 wedges (see Notes)

4 tbsp (56 g) butter, melted

FOR THE BURGER SAUCE

½ cup (120 ml) plain Greek yogurt or mayonnaise

¼ cup (60 ml) barbecue sauce

3 tbsp (45 ml) prepared yellow mustard

1 tbsp (15 ml) ketchup

2 tsp (10 ml) pickle brine

1 tsp chili powder

Preheat the oven to 400°F (204°C).

In a pie pan, whisk together the flour, cheese, paprika, and salt. Pour the milk into another pie pan. Working with one wedge at a time, dip the potatoes in the milk, then into the flour mixture, then lay them on an ungreased half-sheet pan. Drizzle the melted butter over the potatoes. Bake, turning the potatoes over halfway into the cooking time, for 40 to 50 minutes, or until the potatoes are well browned and fork tender.

While the potatoes bake, whisk together all of the ingredients for the burger sauce in a small bowl. Store the sauce, covered, in the refrigerator until the potatoes are ready.

Serve the hot potato wedges with the cold burger sauce and enjoy!

NOTES

You really do need to use Russet potatoes, also known as baking potatoes, for this dish. White, red, and yellow potatoes are not the right texture and will not bake up fluffy.

If possible, use potatoes of roughly the same size, so the wedges will be done in the same amount of time.

HORSERADISH–MUSTARD
Roasted Potatoes

These beautiful roasted potatoes with a flavorful baked-on coating of grainy mustard mixed with horseradish make it the most perfect pairing ever created for roast beef, corned beef, or pot roast.

YIELD: 4 SERVINGS

. . . .

INGREDIENTS

4 large Russet potatoes, peeled or unpeeled, cut in half, then in quarters, then into roughly equal 2–3-inch (5–8-cm) pieces

1 tbsp (18 g) kosher salt

⅓ cup (80 ml) olive oil, divided

3 tbsp (45 ml) whole grain mustard

3 tbsp (45 ml) prepared horseradish

3 tbsp (11 g) chopped fresh parsley

Preheat the oven to 450°F (232°C). Line a baking sheet with heavy-duty foil, dull side up, and set aside.

Place the potatoes in a pot with the salt, cover with water by 1 inch (3 cm), and bring to a boil over high heat. Boil until the potatoes are fork tender, about 10 minutes. Pour the potatoes into a colander and let them air dry for 2 minutes or so, then bang them around a bit by shaking the colander. You want the edges to be a bit rough looking.

Dump the potatoes into a pile on the prepared pan. Drizzle ¼ cup (60 ml) of the oil over the potatoes and toss to coat. Spread the potatoes out on the pan, trying to leave a little space between them.

Roast the potatoes in the preheated oven for 20 minutes, shake the pan, and roast for another 20 to 25 minutes, or until they are crisp-edged and deeply golden brown. While the potatoes roast, whisk together the mustard, horseradish, and remaining oil in a large, heat-proof mixing bowl.

Transfer the potatoes into the bowl with the horseradish mustard mixture, and toss gently to coat before returning to the pan and roasting for 10 more minutes. Serve hot, warm, or at room temperature, garnished with chopped fresh parsley.

NOTE

You can make these with 5 cups (1.6 kg) of leftover Fireman's Chicken Barbecue Salt Potatoes (page 17) that have been halved for a slightly different but equally delicious texture. Simply skip the boiling, but reheat until tender and bang 'em around a bit to soften up the edges.

SPANISH *Tortilla Bites*

These one- or two-bite little potato and egg puffs are a great trick to have up your sleeve. While the word "tortilla" may make you think "taco," this is an homage to "Tortilla Espanola" or a potato egg frittata. It takes one big old potato and yields a whopping 48 bites of these little golden beauties that are a natural alongside soups, stews, salads, and more. Don't worry about having too many, though, they freeze like a dream!

YIELD: 24 SERVINGS (2 EACH)

INGREDIENTS

2 tbsp (30 ml) olive oil

1 large potato, cut into ¼-inch (6-mm) cubes (see Notes)

¾ tsp kosher salt

1 clove of garlic, peeled and minced

4 green onions, roots trimmed and thinly sliced

4 eggs, beaten

½ tsp smoked paprika, for garnish

Preheat the oven to 375°F (190°C).

Heat the oil in a 12-inch (30-cm) skillet over medium heat. Add the potatoes and salt, stirring well to coat the potatoes in oil. Cook for 8 to 10 minutes, stirring frequently, or until the potatoes are tender and lightly browned.

Add in the garlic, stir well, and cook for 1 more minute, or until fragrant. Stir the green onions into the potatoes. Divide the mixture between two 24-cup mini muffin pans or 48 non-stick mini muffin cups. Pour the beaten eggs over the top of the potatoes.

Bake the tortilla bites for 12 minutes, or until puffy and set. Let them stand in the pan for 3 minutes before running a thin, flexible knife around the edge of each tortilla bite and turning them out onto a plate. Put the smoked paprika into a sieve and tap with a spoon to dust the tortilla bites.

NOTES

If you have leftover Fireman's Chicken Barbecue Salt Potatoes (page 17), you can substitute using 2 cups (650 g) of those. Instead of cooking the potatoes for the 8 to 10 minutes specified, just heat the oil as directed above, add the chopped potatoes to the pan, and cook until heated through and slightly browned, about 3 minutes then proceed with the rest of the recipe.

To freeze these for later, let them cool completely to room temperature and freeze on a sheet pan before transferring to a labeled and dated zip-top freezer bag. Wrap the freezer bag with foil to avoid freezer burn, and store for up to 3 months. Take out just as many as you need and reheat in a 350°F (176°C) oven just long enough to warm all the way through, about 15 to 20 minutes.

BROCCOLI

I remember actively disliking broccoli as a kid. It all changed at age 13 when I was served a bowl of cream of broccoli soup by my friend's mother, whose feelings I didn't want to hurt, and realized how amazing it was. All bets were off and I was a broccoli addict from that moment on.

I'm super keen on raw broccoli and cooked broccoli in almost all forms, but I cannot stand overcooked broccoli. I'm banishing bland or mushy broccoli recipes with four spectacular recipes in this chapter.

Spicy Asian Roasted Broccoli (page 32) is my go-to broccoli recipe for almost all meals. Broccoli florets are tossed with a lightly spicy, slightly sweet sauce before being roasted to caramelized, crisp edged perfection. The recipe includes instructions on how to make a much milder, non-Asian inspired version for accompanying other meals. This recipe might be the one you use more than any other broccoli recipe!

I also have a duo of shaved broccoli stem salads. My sister Christina and her best friend Lindsay used to cannibalize all of our broccoli so they could eat the stems, and they were onto something. Shaved into thin strips and tossed with a spicy vinaigrette and crumbled feta or Cotija cheese, the Shaved Broccoli Stem Salad with Mexicali Dressing (page 36) is delicious with tacos, burritos, enchiladas, and much more. The Shaved Broccoli Stem Salad with Feta, Golden Raisins, and Toasted Nuts (page 39) is a little more sophisticated and a natural pairing for all roasted meats, especially lamb and chicken.

SHOPPING TIPS: Look for bright green, firm, compact clusters of florets. More open florets will indicate older broccoli. Stems should be firm and strong, not flexible or rubbery. Fresh broccoli will feel heavy for its size. Avoid broccoli with yellow flowers or dry, brown, or rubbery stalks.

STORAGE: A closed container is the enemy of broccoli storage. Wrap your broccoli gently in paper towels and store in an unsealed plastic bag in the refrigerator so it can breathe. If you purchase it farmers' market fresh, it is not unusual for it to remain fresh for up to 10 days. If you purchase it at a grocery store, look for it to be good for closer to 1 week. The relative freshness of the broccoli makes all the difference in shelf life.

SPICY ASIAN *Roasted Broccoli*

This slightly spicy, slightly sweet broccoli dish is one of the easiest, most satisfying ways to prepare broccoli and is full of concentrated broccoli goodness. It goes fantastically with any grilled, roasted, broiled, or stir-fried beef, chicken, pork, fish, or shrimp that needs a little punchy side dish. Happily, this is delicious when made from either fresh or frozen broccoli with an ever-so-slight adjustment in preparation.

YIELD: 4 SERVINGS

. . . .

INGREDIENTS

2 tbsp (30 ml) grapeseed or canola oil

2 tsp (10 ml) chili-garlic sauce or Sambal Oelek

1 tsp toasted sesame oil

1 tsp light brown sugar

2 cloves of garlic, peeled and thinly sliced

½ tsp kosher salt

4 cups (364 g) fresh or frozen broccoli florets

Sesame seeds and sliced green onions, for garnish, optional

Preheat the oven to 450°F (232°C) with a rack in the middle position. If you're preparing this with fresh broccoli, spray a rimmed half-sheet pan with non-stick cooking spray and set aside. If you're using frozen broccoli, place the rimmed half-sheet pan in the oven to preheat with it.

In a medium-sized bowl combine the grapeseed oil, chili-garlic sauce, sesame oil, sugar, garlic, and salt. When the oven is hot, add the broccoli to the bowl and toss to coat. Spread the broccoli over the prepared pan, making sure there is room for air to circulate around the florets. Roast for 16 to 20 minutes or until the broccoli is crisp-tender and starting to brown around the edges. Garnish with sesame seeds and green onions, if desired. Serve hot, warm, or at room temperature.

NOTE

For a non-Asian style roasted broccoli that is delicious with Cheese Sauce of Champions (page 251), omit the chili-garlic sauce and sesame oil and swap in 1 additional tablespoon (15 ml) of a neutral oil.

CHEESY BROCCOLI *Rice Pancakes*

These may sound a little odd, but I promise it's a side dish you'll turn to time and time again. These savory egg and rice pancakes are packed with fresh broccoli and melted cheese. I'm a big fan of recipes that upcycle odds and ends from the refrigerator into something amazing and these fit the bill! Made from leftover rice, we love these delicious hand-held pancakes served with hearty soups like cream of broccoli (naturally!) and beef stew. They're also a great quick-and-easy, light lunch option.

YIELD: 4 TO 5 SERVINGS

. . . .

INGREDIENTS

1 cup (186 g) chilled leftover white or brown long-grain rice (see Notes)

1 cup (91 g) finely chopped fresh broccoli (see Notes)

3 eggs

½ cup (57 g) shredded cheese (Cheddar, Monterey Jack, or pepper Jack)

2 tsp (10 ml) hot sauce (such as Cholula, Frank's RedHot, or Tabasco)

½ tsp kosher salt

½ tsp freshly ground black pepper

2 tbsp (30 ml) sunflower or canola oil, divided

Sour cream, for dipping, optional

If the chilled rice is clumpy, break it up with your hands. Add the rice to a large mixing bowl. Vigorously stir together the rice, broccoli, eggs, cheese, hot sauce, salt, and pepper to combine it evenly.

Place a 12-inch (30-cm) non-stick skillet over medium-high heat and drizzle about 1 tablespoon (15 ml) of the oil into the pan. Swirl to coat evenly, scoop a scant ¼ cup (60 g) of the broccoli mixture into the pan and gently flatten. Repeat 3 or 4 times, taking care not to crowd the pan. Let the pancakes fry for 2 to 4 minutes on the first side, or until the underside is a beautiful golden brown. Flip the pancakes and cook for another 2 minutes on the second side. Transfer to a plate. Drizzle the rest of the oil in the pan and stir the remaining broccoli mixture before scooping and frying it as you did with the first batch.

Serve hot, warm, or at room temperature by themselves or with sour cream to dip.

NOTES

Definitely start with chilled leftover rice for two reasons. First, it maintains its shape in the final pancakes without falling apart. Second, you don't want to start cooking the egg mixture before you hit the pan, and hot rice will definitely do that, negating the binding power of the egg!

You can opt to use 2 cups (242 g) of leftover roasted broccoli (page 32) in place of the fresh broccoli if you'd like!

SHAVED BROCCOLI STEM *Salad* WITH MEXICALI DRESSING

While my desire to make a broccoli stem salad started with a very "waste not, want not" inspiration, it ended up being something that I love madly. When you're preparing your Spicy Asian Roasted Broccoli (page 32) make sure you save those stems, because you're going to love this salad made from shaved raw broccoli stems with a lime and crumbled cheese dressing that you toss together right in the mixing bowl! Serve this with any Mexican or Tex-Mex inspired main dishes, especially carnitas or beef barbacoa.

YIELD: 4 SERVINGS

. . . .

INGREDIENTS

Leaves and stalks from 2 bunches of broccoli, approximately 4–6 stalks, shaved into thin strips with a vegetable peeler

¼ cup (4 g) fresh cilantro leaves

2 tbsp (30 ml) Luke's Infused Garlic Oil (page 246)

1 tbsp (15 ml) fresh lime juice

¼ tsp ground cumin

¼ tsp chili powder

½ tsp kosher salt

¼ tsp freshly ground black pepper

½ cup (75 g) crumbled feta cheese (Cotija cheese also works well)

Add the broccoli strips and leaves, cilantro, oil, lime juice, cumin, chili powder, salt, and pepper to a bowl and toss to coat. Fold in the cheese and serve immediately.

SHAVED BROCCOLI STEM *Salad* WITH FETA, GOLDEN RAISINS, AND TOASTED NUTS

If you eat broccoli the way we eat broccoli, you'll be thrilled to have a second delectable broccoli stem salad in your repertoire. This salad is sophisticated and studded with crumbled feta cheese, sweet golden raisins, and toasted nuts. Serve this salad with grilled or roasted fish, chicken, or lamb and be prepared for the accolades.

YIELD: 4 SERVINGS

INGREDIENTS

Leaves and stalks from 2 bunches of broccoli, shaved into thin strips with a vegetable peeler

¼ cup (36 g) golden raisins

2 tbsp (30 ml) Luke's Infused Garlic Oil (page 246)

1 tbsp (15 ml) fresh lemon juice

½ tsp fresh lemon zest

½ tsp kosher salt

¼ tsp freshly ground black pepper

½ cup (75 g) crumbled feta

½ cup (73 g) toasted chopped walnuts, slivered almonds, or pine nuts

Add the broccoli strips and leaves, raisins, oil, lemon juice and zest, salt, and pepper to a bowl and toss to coat. Fold in the feta cheese and toasted nuts and serve immediately.

CAULIFLOWER

While cauliflower is getting some respect for its chameleon-like abilities to work with almost any cuisine, people need to know that it can be the vehicle that delivers major flavor, too. Somehow, cauliflower went from a boring, bland vegetable to a low-carb powerhouse vegetable in the past five years. So be gone, boring cauliflower! Every recipe in here delivers a major one-two punch of texture and flavor.

We bring the spicy, tangy flavor that defines The City of Good Neighbors with the Buffalo Cauliflower "Wing" Bites (page 42). Coated with Garlic Buffalo Wing Sauce (page 255), this crispy, crunchy, habit-forming side dish can do triple duty as an appetizer or vegetarian main dish.

Of course, I have to include my kids' favorite take on cauliflower; Bacon-Cheddar Cauliflower Tots (page 46). You can start this one with fresh cauliflower or frozen riced cauliflower, but either way the end result is incredible. Nobody can resist the cauli-tots that are positively bursting with crisp, salty bacon and tremendous quantities of melted Cheddar cheese.

And the humble cauliflower gets a bit of the *My Fair Lady* treatment in the form of Parmesan-Pepper Cauliflower Steaks (page 49). Hearty slabs of cauliflower are brushed with infused garlic oil (page 246), before being roasted and crusted with black pepper and Parmesan cheese. These gorgeously browned, crisp-topped cauliflower steaks are juicy on the inside and visually stunning with a little drizzle of Spinach Pesto Pasta sauce (page 56) or purchased pesto sauce.

SHOPPING TIPS: Look for firm, tightly closed cauliflower with no darkened or off-color spots. White varieties of cauliflower should be very pale and uniformly colored.

STORAGE: Cauliflower is one hearty little cruciferous vegetable. It doesn't take much to keep it happy, but you shouldn't keep it in a sealed bag or package. Keep cauliflower loosely wrapped in plastic in the refrigerator for up to 2 weeks.

Note: Cauliflower is ethylene sensitive.

BUFFALO CAULIFLOWER *"Wing" Bites*

I love cauliflower, but my kids? Well, three out of five of them would say, "Not so much." This oven-baked, crispy-coated, tender cauliflower is an exception to their usual disdain for the white cruciferous vegetable. It's all about the wing sauce because it's a well-known fact that Buffalo wing sauce makes everything tastier. After these cauliflower florets are coated with a simple batter of flour, water, and hot sauce, they are baked to crispy, crunchy perfection and tossed with wing sauce before briefly returning to the oven. Eat them with any grilled, breaded, or roasted chicken or pork, or serve them alone as a vegetarian main dish!

YIELD: 6 SERVINGS AS A SIDE OR 3 AS A MAIN DISH

INGREDIENTS

¾ cup (42 g) unseasoned panko bread crumbs, divided

½ cup (63 g) all-purpose flour (1-for-1 gluten-free flour can be used here)

½ cup (120 ml) water

1 tbsp (15 ml) hot sauce, preferably Frank's RedHot for the most authentic flavor

1 tsp kosher salt

½ tsp ground black pepper

1 medium-sized head of cauliflower, broken into bite-size pieces

2 tbsp (30 ml) Garlic Buffalo Wing Sauce (page 255) or purchased wing sauce, plus more as desired

Thinly-sliced green onions or parsley, for garnish, optional

Blue cheese or ranch dressing, for dipping, optional

Preheat the oven to 450°F (232°C). Line a baking sheet with heavy-duty foil, dull side up, and spray with nonstick cooking spray or brush the pan with oil. Pour ½ cup (28 g) of the panko crumbs onto the prepared pan and set aside.

In a large mixing bowl, whisk together the flour, water, hot sauce, salt, and pepper until smooth. Add the cauliflower florets into the bowl and gently toss to coat thoroughly. Use a slotted spoon to transfer the cauliflower onto the panko on the prepared pan. Scatter the remaining panko over the cauliflower and toss to coat, then spread the florets out so there is some space for air to circulate around them in the oven.

Bake the cauliflower for 20 minutes, or until the coating is set and beginning to brown in places. Use a thin, flexible spatula to transfer the cauliflower to another mixing bowl, toss with the Garlic Buffalo Wing Sauce, and then spread the florets back out on the pan. Bake for 10 minutes, or until the sauce has started to brown in places on the cauliflower.

If desired, drizzle additional wing sauce over the Buffalo Cauliflower "Wing" Bites and serve garnished with green onions and with blue cheese dressing for dipping.

HONEY GARLIC–GLAZED
Cauliflower Bites

These crunchy, baked, honey and garlic–glazed cauliflower bites are ridiculously easy and habit-forming. If you didn't know they were made in the oven, you'd swear they were fried! I nibbled so many of these one time that I was full by the time I got to the table for dinner. They're great with grilled sausages, pork, and chicken or stir-fried meat of any sort. You can serve these as a vegetarian main dish or as an appetizer, too!

YIELD: 6 TO 8 SERVINGS AS A SIDE OR 3 AS A MAIN DISH

INGREDIENTS

¾ cup (42 g) unseasoned panko bread crumbs, divided

½ cup (63 g) all-purpose flour (1-for-1 gluten-free flour can be used here)

½ cup (120 ml) water

1 tsp kosher salt

½ tsp granulated garlic

1 small head cauliflower, broken into roughly even, bite-size florets

⅓ cup (80 ml) mild honey

1 tbsp (15 ml) soy sauce

2 cloves of garlic, peeled and minced or pressed, or 1 tsp garlic paste

1 tsp (5 g) grated fresh ginger or ginger paste

½ tsp crushed red pepper flakes, optional

Thinly sliced green onions, for garnish

Preheat the oven to 450°F (232°C). Line a baking sheet with heavy-duty foil, dull side up, and spray with nonstick cooking spray or brush the pan with oil. Pour ½ cup (28 g) of the panko crumbs onto the prepared pan and set aside.

In a large mixing bowl, whisk together the all-purpose flour, water, salt, and granulated garlic until smooth. Add the cauliflower into the bowl and gently toss to coat thoroughly. Use a slotted spoon to transfer the cauliflower to the prepared pan over the panko crumbs. Scatter the remaining panko over the cauliflower and toss to coat, then spread the florets out so there is some space for air to circulate around them in the oven. Bake for 25 to 30 minutes, or until the cauliflower is tender, and the coating is set and the crumbs are deep golden brown in places.

In a large skillet, combine the honey, soy sauce, garlic, ginger, and crushed red pepper flakes, if using, over high heat and bring it to a boil. Use a slotted spoon to transfer the crispy cauliflower to the skillet and toss gently to coat. Serve garnished with green onions.

Store leftovers tightly wrapped in the refrigerator. You can reheat/re-crisp these by heating briefly in a 350°F (176°C) oven on a greased and foil-covered cookie sheet.

BACON-CHEDDAR *Cauliflower Tots*

It's impossible to underestimate the snackable power these tiny little bites pack. You can start with a fresh head of cauliflower or with convenient frozen riced cauliflower; whatever you have on hand. You add in copious amounts of crispy bacon and sharp Cheddar, some other goodies, then scoop onto a baking sheet and bake 'til the cheese is melted and crunchtastic. These are a great way to get vegetables into picky kids. Trust me. It used to be that three of my five wouldn't touch cauliflower unless it was cooked like this! Serve this with burgers, steaks, pulled pork, and grilled, roasted, or broiled chicken.

YIELD: 8 GENEROUS SERVINGS

INGREDIENTS

2 lbs (907 g) cauliflower florets (see Note to use frozen cauliflower rice)

1½ tsp (9 g) kosher salt, divided

¼ cup (31 g) cornmeal

8 oz (226 g) sharp Cheddar cheese, shredded

12 strips of bacon, cooked until crispy, then crumbled or finely chopped

2 large eggs

1 tsp dried mustard powder

½ tsp granulated garlic

½ tsp granulated onion

½ tsp cayenne pepper

Using a box grater or the standard grating disc on a food processor, grate the cauliflower florets until they are about the size of cooked rice grains. Scrape the grated cauliflower into a bowl lined with a clean kitchen towel. Sprinkle 1 teaspoon of the salt over the top. Let the cauliflower stand at room temperature for 5 minutes, then gather the towel up at the edges, pile the excess towel on top and microwave for 2 minutes. Remove from the microwave, open the towel, and let the cauliflower cool until it is comfortable to handle. Gather up the corners of the towel again, and twist while squeezing the cooked cauliflower to remove as much moisture as possible.

Preheat the oven to 425°F (220°C). Line two half-sheet pans with parchment paper.

Empty any liquid from the bowl you used to microwave the cauliflower and turn the cooked cauliflower into it. Add the remaining salt, cornmeal, cheese, bacon, eggs, mustard powder, granulated garlic and onion, and cayenne pepper and stir vigorously to combine evenly. Use a small cookie scoop to portion out the mixture onto the pan, leaving about 1½ inches (4 cm) between the tots to allow for spreading while they bake. Gently pat the tots to flatten slightly.

Bake the tots for 25 minutes, or until golden brown on top, and darker deep brown on the underside. Let the tots stand on the pan for 2 minutes before transferring to a serving plate.

NOTE

To make the tots from frozen cauliflower rice, line a microwave safe bowl with a clean, cotton kitchen towel. Pour the frozen cauliflower rice into the towel-lined bowl. Sprinkle 1 teaspoon of the kosher salt over the top. Let this stand at room temperature for 5 minutes, then gather the towel up at the edges, pile the excess towel on top, and microwave for 4 minutes. Proceed with squeezing as directed above.

PARMESAN-PEPPER
Cauliflower Steaks

Impressive looking and oh-so-tasty with a golden-brown, crisp crust, these deceptively simple cauliflower "steaks" banish thoughts of boring cauliflower forever. Pair these with, well, anything! They do go especially nicely with chicken, pork, and sausage, but they also stand alone as a vegetarian main dish.

YIELD: 8 SERVINGS AS A SIDE DISH, 4 SERVINGS AS A MAIN DISH

INGREDIENTS

2 heads of cauliflower (about 2 lbs [907 g] each), outer leaves removed, stem trimmed

¼ cup (60 ml) olive oil

1 tsp kosher salt

¾ tsp cracked black pepper

½ tsp granulated garlic

½ tsp smoked paprika or sweet paprika

½ cup (50 g) grated Parmesan cheese

½ cup (120 ml) Spinach Pesto Pasta sauce (page 56) or store-bought pesto

Preheat the oven to 500°F (260°C).

Use a large knife to cut the cauliflower heads in half lengthwise through the center. Lay the cauliflower cut side down and cut the halves in half lengthwise again before cutting a 1½-inch (4-cm) thick slab from each quarter of the cauliflower. (See Notes for what to do with the rest of the cauliflower.) Place the cauliflower slabs on a rimmed half-sheet pan.

Drizzle the olive oil evenly over both sides of the cauliflower steaks, using a pastry brush to distribute it, if desired.

Use a fork or small whisk to combine the salt, black pepper, granulated garlic, and paprika and sprinkle that evenly over both sides of the cauliflower. Cover with foil and cinch it around the pan. Bake for 5 minutes.

Remove the foil and roast for 10 minutes before gently flipping and sprinkling with the grated Parmesan. Return the steaks to the oven for another 6 to 8 minutes. Serve with pesto sauce on the side.

NOTES

If your cauliflower is quite large, you may be able to sneak another slab out of each one. Otherwise, use florets that don't make it into a steak for Bacon-Cheddar Cauliflower Tots (page 46), Buffalo Cauliflower "Wing" Bites (page 42), or Honey Garlic–Glazed Cauliflower Bites (page 45).

Use fresh grated and not powdered Parmesan cheese in this recipe.

This recipe is a blueprint for fun. Try omitting the Parmesan cheese and adding a teaspoon of curry powder to the spice mix for a gorgeous side dish for curries.

SPINACH

Spinach and I are fast friends. I love it raw, cooked, and everywhere in between. Included here are my four all-time favorite ways to use the vegetable that makes Popeye strong-of-arm, and me weak-of-knee.

Before you go any further, try out the Spinach, Bacon, and Cheddar Munchy Cakes (page 52). These hold the distinction of being the first food full of spinach that most of my kids have voluntarily tried, as you can probably tell from the name they gave it, and for good reason. Everyone loves finger food and these savory little cakes fit the bill. Pair these with soups, stews, chilis, and chicken dishes.

Spanakorizo (Greek Spinach Rice, page 55) is one of my all-time favorite, all-purpose side dishes. It goes with grilled, baked, roasted, or broiled fish, chicken, pork, or beef, and leftovers are wonderful for lunch. This is another side dish that can make the leap to main dish with the addition of chopped, leftover grilled or roasted chicken.

SHOPPING TIPS: When shopping for mature spinach look for spinach that is crisp, firm, and dark green. For baby spinach, you want tender, loosely packed containers of healthy, dark green leaves. They should not be at all wilted or wet. Avoid limp and yellowing leaves with either mature or baby spinach. Mature spinach is usually better in cooked applications while baby spinach is best when used in a recipe where you're using it raw.

STORAGE: Store in a loose plastic bag (not sealed!) in the refrigerator for about 4 days.

SPINACH, BACON, AND CHEDDAR
Munchy Cakes

When bacon, Cheddar, and spinach come together in these savory snack cakes, smiles are inevitable. You can use fresh spinach or frozen spinach for these, so these are a great option year round. Even the pickiest eaters tuck into these with gusto! We love these with soups, stews, chilis, and grilled, broiled, or roast chicken.

YIELD: 8 SERVINGS

INGREDIENTS

1 lb (454 g) fresh or frozen spinach

3 cups (339 g) shredded Cheddar cheese

1½ cups (162 g) fine bread crumbs

6 large eggs

½ lb (226 g) of bacon, cooked, drained, crumbled, or finely chopped

¼ tsp dry mustard powder

Hot sauce, for serving, optional

Preheat the oven to 375°F (190°C). Line a baking sheet (or two, depending on size) with parchment paper.

If you're using fresh spinach, drop your spinach (leaves, stems, and all) into a pot of salted, rapidly boiling water for 40 seconds, then use tongs or a slotted spoon to transfer them to a bowl of ice water to stop the cooking process. After the spinach is cold, drain it and then squeeze it to remove as much moisture as possible.

If you're using frozen spinach, thaw it first, then drain and squeeze it to remove as much excess moisture as possible.

Roughly chop the spinach, then stir the spinach, Cheddar cheese, bread crumbs, eggs, bacon, and mustard powder together until even. Scoop about ¼ to ⅓ cup (60 to 80 g) of the mixture (an amount about equal to the size of a plum) and form into a patty. Place the patties on the prepared pan. Repeat until all of the mixture is formed into patties.

Bake for 25 to 30 minutes, flipping the patties after about 15 minutes, until they are all golden brown and crisp on the outside.

Serve hot, warm, or cool with your preferred hot sauce.

SPANAKOPITA *Dip*

Can you call a dip a side dish? Well, you can when the dip is so full of spinach that Popeye would approve. I don't just serve this as a dip for pita bread, chips or vegetables, I also use it to top grilled chicken, fish, and as a spread for sandwiches or flatbread.

YIELD: 12 SERVINGS

INGREDIENTS

2 tbsp (30 ml) Luke's Infused Garlic Oil (page 246) or extra-virgin olive oil

1 small onion, diced

1 tsp kosher salt

3 cloves of garlic, peeled and minced

1 (17.6-ounce [482-g]) container of plain Greek yogurt

1 lb (454 g) frozen chopped spinach, thawed and lightly squeezed to remove excess moisture

1 cup (150 g) feta cheese crumbles

½ cup (30 g) packed fresh parsley leaves and tender stems, finely minced (or 3 tbsp [6 g] dried parsley flakes)

2 tbsp (6 g) minced fresh dill weed (or 2 tsp [2 g] dried dill weed)

Drizzle the oil into a small skillet over medium heat. Add the onion and salt and stir to coat the onion in oil. Sweat the onion, stirring frequently, until translucent and crisp tender, about 4 minutes. If the onion shows signs of browning, reduce the heat.

Add the garlic, stir in well, and cook for 1 minute more, or until fragrant. Stir thoroughly together with the yogurt, spinach, feta cheese, and herbs and transfer to a tightly-covered container. Refrigerate for at least 1 hour before serving to give the flavors a chance to meld. This dip is good for a week in the refrigerator.

TOMATOES

Tomato season is the best, isn't it? I love all tomatoes from the ruby-red, juicy beefsteak beauties to the muted colors but far-from-muted flavors of the heirloom varieties that are meant for eating sliced and fresh. Plum a.k.a. Roma tomatoes are a wonderful all-purpose variety that is great for fresh salads and cooking down to make sauce. And who doesn't love poppingly fresh cherry tomatoes?

Meaty plum tomatoes have star power in the simple-to-prepare but memorable Parmesan-Baked Tomatoes (page 62) topped with garlicky, herbed fresh bread crumbs and baked just until hot all the way through. It's amazing how robust something so easy and pared down can taste.

Tomatoes get another blockbuster turn in the Whipped Feta–Stuffed Cherry Tomatoes (page 65) that features bite-size, burstingly ripe tomatoes stuffed with a fluffy, creamy, utterly celestial, roasted garlic whipped feta that's good enough to keep making even when tomato season is merely a winter fireside dream. Psst. You can keep stuffing cherry tomatoes year round with greenhouse tomatoes!

Movie lovers will dig Tomato Inception (page 69), this dream within a dream of a tomato side dish features not one, not two, but three different forms of tomatoes; fresh (or canned), tomato paste, and sun-dried tomatoes topped with a fabulous layer of cheese filling and crispy, garlicky bread crumbs. My husband rapturously described it as being like a pimento cheese topped tomato pie.

SHOPPING TIPS: Choose semi-firm tomatoes that "give" slightly to gentle pressure from your finger. Do not buy moldy, soft, or bruised tomatoes.

STORAGE: If you end up with some under-ripe tomatoes, you can put them on the counter in a loosely closed paper bag. Check daily until they are ripe. For ripe tomatoes, store in a cool, dark place (not the refrigerator!) stem side down and use within 3 days. If they are ripe and you're not quite ready to use them, you can transfer them to the refrigerator for another couple of days, but you will lose some of the intensity of a room temperature fresh tomato.

PARMESAN-*Baked Tomatoes*

Have you ever been overrun with tomatoes when they're in season? It's such a lovely problem to have, but you need strategies to use up the abundance, and this one should be near the top of your list. Herbed Parmesan bread crumbs are piled high on fresh tomatoes and baked just until hot and are incredible served with grilled steaks, pork chops, or chicken. While I like these best made with in-season tomatoes, I have certainly made them with some good greenhouse tomatoes year round and been very happy!

YIELD: 6 SERVINGS

· ·

INGREDIENTS

6 plum tomatoes, halved

2 slices of bread (see Notes)

¼ tsp kosher salt

¼ tsp coarsely ground black pepper

½ cup (50 g) grated Parmesan cheese

¼ cup (15 g) finely chopped fresh herbs (see Notes)

Preheat the oven to 400°F (204°C).

Arrange the tomatoes, cut side up, in a 9 x 13-inch (23 x 33-cm) baking dish.

Add the bread, salt, and pepper to a blender or food processor fitted with a metal blade. Pulse a few times until you have coarse fresh bread crumbs with no pieces larger than a small green pea. Transfer the crumbs to a bowl and use a fork to combine them with the cheese and herbs. Divide the crumb topping between the tomatoes and bake for 10 minutes, or until the tomatoes are hot all the way through and the crumb topping is golden brown on top.

If your tomatoes are hot, but the crumb topping hasn't browned yet, you can simply pop it under the broiler for a few seconds. It's better to do that than to keep baking because you want the tomatoes to maintain their structural integrity; not to become mushy.

NOTES

You can use sandwich bread or sturdier sourdough or Italian bread. All of them will yield slightly different but equally delicious results!

My favorite combination of herbs is whatever I have in the house! Usually this is parsley, chives (or green onion tops), basil, or cilantro. Try to use herbs that go together usually for the most harmonious results. Think basil plus parsley, chives plus dill and parsley, parsley plus cilantro, etc. . . .

WHIPPED FETA—STUFFED
Cherry Tomatoes

Put your pinkies up; these little one-bite cherry tomato halves filled with roasted garlic–whipped feta cheese are going to be your new favorite elegant side dish in the summer! They look and taste great next to grilled chicken, fish, and steak and any leftover whipped feta makes an excellent sandwich spread or dip for raw vegetables.

YIELD: 8 SERVINGS

INGREDIENTS

8 oz (226 g) feta cheese crumbles brought to room temperature

4 oz (113 g) cream cheese

4–8 cloves of roasted garlic either purchased or homemade (see Note)

1 pint (298 g) cherry tomatoes, halved and then seeds and juices scooped out

1 tbsp (3 g) snipped chives and/or 1 tbsp (4 g) minced fresh parsley, for garnish

Add the feta to the bowl of a food processor fitted with a metal blade. Pulse the feta until it is completely broken up into sandy crumbs. Add the cream cheese and garlic to the bowl and process, stopping to scrape down the sides occasionally, until the mixture is velvety smooth, creamy, and warm, about 4 to 5 minutes. Scrape the mixture into a jar with a tight-fitting lid and refrigerate until it is cool all the way through, about 2 hours.

Let the tomatoes rest, cut side down, on a plate or cutting board lined with a double thickness of paper towels while you scoop half of the whipped feta mixture into a large, zip-top freezer bag. Squeeze the cheese spread into one corner of the bag, squeeze out as much air as possible, and seal the bag. Work the mixture a little with your hands until it is soft. Snip the end of the bag off and pipe the cheese into the hollows of the tomatoes. Garnish with chives and/or parsley.

NOTE

To roast your own garlic, preheat the oven to 400°F (204°C). Slice the top off of a head of garlic to expose the cloves. Place on a large square of foil in a small baking dish and drizzle with ¼ cup (60 ml) of olive oil. Sprinkle it with an ⅛ teaspoon each of kosher salt and black pepper before cinching the foil up around it and baking for 40 minutes or until the garlic is soft and golden. Squeeze the cloves out and use it on EVERYTHING!

HEAVENLY BLISTERED
Cherry Tomatoes

You'll never again curse the crazy amounts of cherry tomatoes you find in your CSA share or garden because WHOA are these good. This ultra-simple side dish is the heavenly combination of cherry tomatoes cooked briefly in an ultra-hot, cast-iron pan with a little oil until the skins of the tomatoes blister and they pop. A little thinly sliced garlic is added, then at the very end, a shower of thinly sliced basil and shaved Parmesan gilds this blistered tomato lily. I can eat these just about any which way, from being spooned over or next to a beautiful steak or roasted chicken, to being chilled and spooned on top of cottage cheese for a light lunch. It's also delicious over ricotta cheese topped toast.

YIELD: 4 SERVINGS

• •

INGREDIENTS

2 tbsp (30 ml) sunflower or pure light olive oil

3 cups (447 g) cherry tomatoes

4 cloves of garlic, thinly sliced

6 leaves of fresh Italian basil, thinly sliced

¾ tsp Maldon sea salt flakes (or ½ tsp coarse kosher salt)

¾ tsp freshly ground black pepper

¼ cup (25 g) grated Parmesan cheese, for garnish

Place an 8- to 10-inch (20- to 25-cm) cast-iron skillet over high heat. Drizzle the oil in the pan and heat until it is shimmery and almost ready to smoke. Carefully add in the tomatoes and let them stand in the pan without moving the pan for 3 minutes. The tomatoes will be spluttery and will pop. After 3 minutes, stir with a long-handled spoon or shimmy the pan carefully, then cook for 1 more minute.

Drop the heat to low and stir in the garlic. Cook for 1 additional minute, then remove from the heat. Stir in the basil. Sprinkle with salt and pepper, and garnish with the Parmesan cheese.

Store leftovers tightly lidded in the refrigerator for up to a week.

NOTES

If you have leftover Heavenly Blistered Cherry Tomatoes, you can serve them as is or pureed over pasta for a flavorful, fast pasta sauce or add them to soups.

Maldon sea salt flakes are large, thin, uneven, crunchy, clean-tasting salt flakes meant for finishing food. If you cannot find this, you can substitute other sea salt flakes, but do so to taste.

Tomato INCEPTION

This tomato dish is like the concept from the movie *Inception*: a dream within a dream within a dream. Bursting with a variety of forms of tomato like fresh (or canned) diced tomatoes, tomato paste, and sun-dried tomatoes, all covered with a cheesy melted topping plus garlicky, crunchy bread crumbs, this herb-studded casserole is one you'll want over and over. My husband described this as being like pimento cheese plus tomato pie. Make this on repeat during fresh tomato season, but don't forget about it in the cold weather months too! Serve with all chicken and pork dishes!

YIELD: 8 SERVINGS

- -

INGREDIENTS

6 plum or Roma tomatoes (or 1 quart [960 ml] canned diced tomatoes, drained)

½ tsp kosher salt

1 cup (160 g) diced onion

3 cloves of garlic, peeled and thinly sliced

¼ cup (14 g) sun-dried tomatoes packed in oil, drained, finely chopped

2 tbsp (32 g) tomato paste

6–8 large leaves fresh basil, stacked, rolled up, and thinly sliced into strips

½ tsp dried thyme

1 cup (113 g) shredded extra sharp Cheddar cheese

1 cup (112 g) shredded mozzarella cheese

½ cup (120 ml) mayonnaise

2 tsp (10 ml) hot sauce (like Frank's RedHot, Tabasco, or Cholula)

½ cup (28 g) panko bread crumbs

1 tbsp (15 ml) garlic or regular extra-virgin olive oil

Preheat the oven to 350°F (176°C).

If using plum or Roma tomatoes, slice them in half and use your fingers to scoop out the seeds and liquid centers of the tomatoes. Squeeze gently to remove more liquid. Dice the tomatoes into ¼- to ½-inch (6- to 12-mm) pieces and toss with the kosher salt. Add the tomatoes to a colander and toss every 5 minutes while the oven preheats. When the oven reaches the correct temperature, squeeze the tomatoes to remove as much liquid as you can without totally destroying the tomatoes.

Scatter the diced onion and sliced garlic over the bottom of an 8 x 8–inch (20 x 20–cm) square baking dish or casserole dish. In a large mixing bowl, toss the diced tomatoes, sun-dried tomatoes, tomato paste, basil, and thyme together until even and scatter over the onions and garlic.

In a small mixing bowl, stir together the Cheddar and mozzarella cheese, mayonnaise, and hot sauce vigorously until evenly combined, then dollop over the tomatoes and spread evenly to the edges of the pan. In another small mixing bowl, toss together the bread crumbs and olive oil and scatter over the top of the cheese. Bake the casserole for 45 minutes, or until the cheese is bubbly and the bread crumbs are golden brown.

Use a spatula to transfer the lovely tomatoes to a serving plate and serve!

RED, WHITE, AND BLEU CHEESE
Salad

The red is from the tomatoes, the white is from white balsamic vinegar, and the bleu cheese is self-explanatory in this salad that is so good it'll make you want to salute. We serve this on repeat at our house all summer long. It comes together in five minutes or less, tastes dreamy, and goes with anything and everything grilled.

YIELD: 4 SERVINGS

. . . .

INGREDIENTS

4 ripe beefsteak tomatoes or 6 plum tomatoes, sliced into ¼-inch (6-mm) thick slices

1 tbsp (15 ml) Luke's Infused Garlic or Parsley Oil (page 246) or extra-virgin olive oil

2 tsp (10 ml) white balsamic vinegar (see Notes)

¼ cup (34 g) bleu cheese crumbles

2 tsp (3 g) finely minced fresh parsley (chives or green onion tops can also be used)

½ tsp coarse Maldon sea salt flakes (see Notes)

½ tsp coarsely ground black pepper

Arrange the tomato slices so they're slightly overlapping on a serving dish. Drizzle the oil and vinegar over the top. Scatter the bleu cheese crumbles followed by the herbs, salt, and pepper. Serve immediately.

NOTES

White balsamic vinegar is milder and slightly less sweet than classic balsamic vinegar, and it has a beautiful pale golden color. It is wonderful in this recipe, but if you can't find it, you can substitute classic balsamic vinegar in an equal amount.

Maldon sea salt flakes are large, thin, uneven, crunchy, clean-tasting salt flakes meant for finishing food. If you cannot find this, you can substitute other sea salt flakes, but do so to taste.

ZUCCHINI
(or Summer Squash)

During zucchini season, it's hard to take a step without tripping over a summer squash. In fact, my Amish neighbors have been known to prank each other by hiding femur-sized zucchini on each other's buggies while visiting each other. Thankfully, I have four rock-star recipes that will keep you happily consuming the super-abundant vegetable.

Kick it off with Papa's Zucchini Patties (page 74); a bullet-proof recipe from my dad that kept his (at the time) vegetarian kids happy. Now as a committed omnivore, I still enthusiastically devour these crispy-edged, tender zucchini patties.

Crispy Baked Zucchini Fries (page 78) are like the gateway drug of zucchini consumption. Seasoned panko crumbs coat these zucchini fries that bake to perfection and are great dunked into marinara sauce, ketchup, or Smoked Paprika Chipotle Sauce (page 252).

If you can lay your hands on baby zucchini, please do for Garlicky Grilled Zucchini with Lemons (page 77), where infused oil is brushed over zucchini and a halved lemon before they spend very little time on the grill. If you play your cards right and match this with grilled meat, you may not have to spend any time at all that night over a stove!

For all of the recipes in this chapter, you can swap in yellow squash when zucchini is called for if you prefer it or have it on hand.

SHOPPING TIPS: Handle zucchini and other summer squash carefully, because it is delicate and easy to damage. Look for shiny, firm, plump, unwrinkled, heavy-for-its-size squash with deeply-colored skin. Summer squash (and zucchini) is at its best when it is no more than 8-inches (20-cm) long (or 4-inches [10-cm] across if you're considering patty pan squash), but bigger squash are ideal for Papa's Zucchini Patties (page 74) and zucchini bread.

STORAGE: Store unwashed zucchini in a plastic bag in the crisper drawer of your refrigerator for up to 1 week, checking it daily. If the skin becomes wrinkled, use it immediately.

PAPA'S *Zucchini Patties*

Back when I was a teenager—way back, thank you very much—I was a vegetarian. My dad humored me and found a couple of go-to recipes he could make to keep his hungry teenaged vegetarian fed. These crispy-on-the-outside, tender-on-the-inside zucchini patties packed with cheese and onion were one shining example of his cookery. Inexpensive, easy to make, and deliciously satisfying, they make a great side dish for anything at all that's coming off of the grill, roasted chicken, and can, as my dad taught me, even be served between buns for a vegetarian main dish!

YIELD: 5 SERVINGS

INGREDIENTS

3 cups (372 g) coarsely shredded zucchini, about 3 small- to medium-sized zucchini

1 onion, peeled and shredded

1 tsp kosher salt

1 cup (112 g) shredded mozzarella

½ cup (50 g) grated Parmesan or Romano cheese

¼ cup (14 g) panko bread crumbs

¼ cup (31 g) all-purpose flour

2 eggs, lightly beaten

¾ tsp Italian seasoning

½ tsp ground black pepper

¼ tsp granulated garlic

Marinara sauce or sour cream, optional

Minced fresh herbs, optional

Preheat the oven to 400°F (204°C). Line a rimmed half-sheet pan with parchment paper.

Shred the zucchini and onion using a box grater or the grating blade of a food processor. Line a colander with a kitchen towel (see Note), add in the zucchini and onion, then toss with the salt. Let it stand for just as long as it takes you to mix together the mozzarella and Parmesan cheese, bread crumbs, flour, eggs, Italian seasoning, pepper, and granulated garlic in a large mixing bowl.

Position the colander over a bowl or sink, draw together the edges of the towel, and twist to squeeze as much moisture as you can from the mixture. Add the squeezed zucchini and onion to the cheese mixture and stir until evenly combined.

Use a portion scoop, or your hands, to divide the mixture into 10 portions, then form each portion into a patty and space them out on the sheet pan. Bake for 20 minutes, flip, and bake for another 15 minutes, or until deeply golden brown and crispy. Garnish with marinara sauce or sour cream and fresh herbs, if desired.

NOTE

You can skip the kitchen towel step if you're committed to squeezing the life out of the zucchini and onions with your hands. After tossing with the salt and standing, squeeze one handful at a time.

GARLICKY *Grilled Zucchini* WITH LEMONS

Over and over again I'm reminded that my favorite foods are the ones I don't have to fuss over much. I'm not saying that foodstuffs that require effort aren't wonderful, but I'm saying that the ones that surprise me with their perfection are the ones that took five ingredients or less and just a couple of minutes. Case in point, this recipe for Garlicky Grilled Zucchini with Lemons. You start with tender, young zucchini, a halved lemon, olive oil, salt, and pepper. Grill it all up, pop it on a plate, and voilà! Side dish bliss. When all you have is 10 minutes to deliver a great side dish, this is the dish you need.

YIELD: 4 SERVINGS

INGREDIENTS

1 tbsp (15 ml) canola, sunflower, or grapeseed oil for the grill

1 lb (454 g) baby zucchini, whole or small zucchini, quartered lengthwise

2 tbsp (30 ml) Luke's Infused Garlic Oil (page 246) or extra-virgin olive oil

1 tsp kosher salt

½ tsp coarsely ground black pepper

1 whole lemon, scrubbed, then halved

Preheat the grill to high heat. Fold a paper towel into a small square, soak up the canola oil with it, and hold it with tongs while wiping on the hot grill.

In a mixing bowl, toss the zucchini with the infused oil, salt, and pepper. Use tongs to transfer the zucchini to the grill. Slide the cut sides of the lemon around in the bowl to mop up the remaining oil, salt, and pepper to the best of your ability. Put the lemons, cut side down, on the hottest part of the grill and do not move them.

Flip the zucchini every so often, getting grill marks all around if possible, and remove them when they are crisp-tender, about 5 to 6 minutes total. Transfer the zucchini to a serving plate or platter. Gently remove the lemon from the grill, taking care not to squeeze out all the juice over the grill. Place it charred side up on the zucchini and squeeze over the dish right when served.

CRISPY BAKED *Zucchini Fries*

I am clearly a big fan of vegetables served as fries (see Garlicky Baked Asparagus Fries [page 126]), but I want to remove any remaining doubt with this summer favorite. Tender young zucchini are especially good for this recipe, as they don't have many seeds to get in the way of pure zucchini fry enjoyment. If you do use a more mature zucchini, just scrape the seeds out of the center before dividing into fry-sized segments. Serve these with burgers, hot dogs, sausages, grilled chicken, or pork chops.

YIELD: 8 SERVINGS

INGREDIENTS

1 cup (56 g) panko bread crumbs

¾ cup (75 g) freshly-grated Parmesan cheese

2 tsp (5 g) Old Bay seasoning

1½ tsp (3 g) granulated garlic

1 tsp paprika or smoked paprika

½ tsp freshly ground black pepper

2 eggs, beaten

½ cup (63 g) all-purpose flour

1½ lbs (680 g) tender, young zucchini, sliced into ½ x ½ x 3-inch (12 x 12 x 7-mm) strips (see Note)

Preheat the oven to 425°F (220°C). Lightly spray a half-sheet pan with non-stick cooking spray and set aside.

In a pie plate, use a fork to toss together the bread crumbs, cheese, Old Bay, granulated garlic, paprika, and pepper.

Whisk the eggs in another pie plate until evenly colored. Add the all-purpose flour to a dinner plate.

Working with one piece of zucchini at a time, slide it through the flour, shake off the excess, slide it through the eggs, lift to let the excess egg drain away, and then press it into the bread crumb mixture. Flip the zucchini over and press the other side into the crumbs, then transfer it to the prepared half-sheet pan. Repeat with the remaining zucchini strips. Do not crowd the pan.

Bake for 30 to 35 minutes, flipping the fries about 15 minutes through, until golden brown and crispy. Let the fries rest on the pan for 3 to 5 minutes before serving.

NOTE

There is no need to peel the zucchini before slicing it. I think the green looks nice and it adds nutritive value to the zucchini fries!

SUMMER *Sauté*

When your garden is really and truly cranking out the produce and you have zucchini and bell peppers coming out of your ears, this Summer Sauté will save your sanity and please your taste buds at the same time. The only work involved in this dish is cutting up a few vegetables, cooking them just long enough in a skillet and then tossing it all together for a summer-on-a-plate side dish that pairs well with anything on the grill!

YIELD: 6 SERVINGS

. . . .

INGREDIENTS

3 tsp (15 ml) Luke's Infused Garlic Oil (page 246) or extra-virgin olive oil, divided

1 red bell pepper, stem and seeds removed, diced into ½-inch (13-mm) cubes

1 yellow bell pepper, stem and seeds removed, diced into ½-inch (13-mm) cubes

¾ tsp kosher salt, divided

1 small onion, peeled and diced into ½-inch (13-mm) cubes

2 cloves of garlic, thinly sliced

1 tender zucchini, stem removed, diced into ½-inch (13-mm) cubes

2 tbsp (30 ml) red wine vinegar

6 leaves of fresh Italian basil, thinly sliced

Drizzle 1 teaspoon of the oil in a 12-inch (30-cm) skillet over high heat and swirl the pan to coat the bottom. Toss in the bell peppers with ¼ teaspoon of the salt. Stir fry the peppers until crisp tender, about 2 to 3 minutes. Transfer to a heat-proof bowl.

Return the pan to the heat, drizzle in another teaspoon of oil, toss in the onion, garlic, and another ¼ teaspoon of salt. Stir fry until the onion is crisp tender and translucent, about 2 to 3 minutes. Transfer the onion to the bowl with the peppers.

Return the pan to the heat one more time, drizzle in the remaining teaspoon of oil, toss in the zucchini and remaining ¼ teaspoon of salt. Stir fry for 3 minutes, or until the zucchini cubes are hot all the way through and they have a little color but still have some body to them. Add the red wine vinegar to the pan and stir well, scraping the pan. Transfer the zucchini to the bowl with the peppers and onions. Toss in the basil and serve.

CUCUMBERS

When I tell you I love cucumbers, please understand I'm saying "love" loudly with a long, drawn out "o" sound and starry eyes. While I am content to eat them out of hand with just a sprinkle of salt, some meals require a little more to it and cucumbers are a pretty easy way to deliver visual and taste appeal.

At our house, Sriracha-Sesame Cucumber Rice Noodles (page 84) are always well received. The slightly spicy sesame-sriracha is tossed with green onions and al dente rice noodles before getting a shower of toasted sesame seeds and a crown of shaved, refreshing cucumber.

If you're looking for a fast, fabulous, and vibrant side dish for grilled meats or fish, look no further than Cucumber Salad with Blueberries and Feta (page 87). It'll take you longer to slice the cucumbers than to toss together the rest of the dish and it is so good.

And finally, Nana's Cucumbers in Yummy Sauce (page 92) has been a staple side dish that I've loved my whole life. My mom (Nana) served this dish when I was little and I still serve this retro crowd pleaser all summer long!

SHOPPING TIPS: Look for firm, evenly colored cucumbers with no soft or pale spots. English cucumbers (my favorite for all-purpose eating year round) are most often found tightly wrapped in plastic wrap. Slicing cucumbers will be dark green in color and should be mostly smooth. They are often waxed to help extend their shelf life. Pickling cucumbers should be very fresh—ideally picked the same day—and will be small and may be a bit spiky.

STORAGE: English cucumbers which are sweeter with thinner skins should be stored in the refrigerator in the plastic wrap in which they were purchased. They'll be good for up to 10 days.

Slicing cucumbers deliver the classic fresh cucumber flavor we all remember and can be stored at cool room temperature for up to a week.

Pickling cucumbers are smaller, thicker skinned, and have some spines when fresh and should be used the same day they're purchased or picked.

Cucumbers are extremely ethylene sensitive

SRIRACHA–SESAME CUCUMBER
Rice Noodles

May I make a confession? Sometimes I plan entire meals around making this side dish. It's beyond simple; don't let the length of the ingredients list daunt you. You cook noodles, shave a cucumber with a vegetable peeler, and whisk together some sauce then toss it all together. It couldn't get easier than that unless you ordered takeout. But, oh the results! We're talking about tender rice noodles that soak up a flavorful sesame, green onion, and sriracha sauce topped with strips of cooling cucumber strips. I adore this with all fish and chicken dishes and have even used it under stir-fry from time to time.

YIELD: 6 SERVINGS

INGREDIENTS

1 (14-oz [396-g]) package Asian-style rice noodles (see Notes)

3 tbsp (45 ml) low-sodium soy sauce

3 tbsp (45 ml) toasted sesame oil

1–3 tsp (5–15 ml) Sriracha, depending on your heat preference

1 tbsp (15 ml) ketchup

1 tbsp (15 ml) rice wine vinegar

2 cloves of garlic, peeled and minced or pressed with a garlic press

4 green onions, roots removed, thinly sliced, divided

2 tsp (6 g) toasted sesame seeds, divided

1 cucumber, shaved into thin strips with a vegetable peeler (see Notes)

Prepare the rice noodles according to package directions. Drain and rinse the noodles under cold water to stop the cooking.

In a large mixing bowl, whisk together the soy sauce, sesame oil, Sriracha, ketchup, vinegar, and garlic. Add the cooked noodles to the bowl along with the green onions and sesame seeds (reserving 1 tablespoon [3 g] of the green onions and ½ teaspoon of the sesame seeds for garnish) and toss to coat evenly. Top the noodles with the shaved cucumber and garnish with the remaining green onion and sesame seeds.

NOTES

I use broad rice noodles (often sold as Pho noodles) for this salad, but most Asian-style rice noodles will work well.

If using an English (or seedless) cucumber, you do not need to peel the cucumber first. Waxed or slicing cucumbers should be peeled before shaving.

You can make the noodles in sauce up to 3 days ahead of time and then stir and shave the cucumber just before serving. Leftovers are best stored when the cucumber and noodles are stored separately as the cucumbers have less staying power after being shaved.

Cucumber Salad
WITH BLUEBERRIES AND FETA

It sounds weird, right? But I tell you this, it is the most perfectly light, savory with a hint of sweet, easy salad to accompany any chicken or fish entree you have planned. The popping freshness of blueberries and cucumbers is amplified by a simple dressing of fresh mint, white wine vinegar, and garlic extra-virgin olive oil. It comes together in a heart-beat and is surprisingly habit-forming. I love it with both feta and goat cheese, so pick whichever dings your chimes.
Serve this with grilled or roasted chicken or fish.

YIELD: 8 SERVINGS

INGREDIENTS

1 English (seedless) cucumber

1 cup (148 g) fresh blueberries

1 cup (150 g) crumbled feta or goat cheese

6–8 fresh mint leaves, thinly sliced (see Note)

¼ cup (60 ml) Luke's Infused Garlic Oil (page 246) or extra-virgin olive oil

⅛ cup (30 ml) white wine vinegar

1 tsp kosher salt

½ tsp freshly ground black pepper

Peel the cucumber, split lengthwise, and scrape out any seeds that are in your otherwise seedless cucumber. Cut the cucumber into ¼- to ½-inch (6- to 13-mm) slices. In a mixing bowl, add the cucumber, blueberries, feta, mint, oil, vinegar, salt, and pepper and toss together. It can be served immediately or refrigerated for up to 24 hours.

NOTE

The best way to thinly slice an herb like mint is to stack the leaves and roll them up like a cigar, then slice thinly across the roll of leaves. This works for sage and basil as well.

CUCUMBER *Kimchi*

Cucumber Kimchi somehow manages to be spicy and cooling all at the same time. Full of umami flavor, you may find this crunchy, refreshing Korean summertime staple to be habit forming with grilled beef, chicken, pork, and fish dishes. It only lasts 7 days in the refrigerator, but if you manage to stretch it that far, you have far more self-control than I do. Thankfully, it's simple to make!

YIELD: 6 TO 8 SERVINGS

. . . .

INGREDIENTS

1 lb (454 g) pickling cucumbers or seedless cucumbers, cut into 2-inch (5-cm) long sections, then quartered lengthwise

1 tbsp (18 g) kosher salt

2 tbsp (12 g) Korean chili flakes (gochugaru)

1 tbsp (6 g) minced fresh garlic (not jarred)

1 tbsp (15 g) grated apple or pear

1 tbsp (15 g) granulated sugar (or mild honey)

1 tsp fish sauce

½ tsp grated fresh ginger (not jarred or ginger puree from a tube)

4 green onions, roots trimmed, cut in half lengthwise and then into 2-inch (5-cm) sections

1 small carrot, scrubbed and trimmed, shaved into thin strips with a vegetable peeler

Add the cucumbers to a bowl with the salt and toss gently with your hands to coat. Let the cucumbers rest at room temperature for 30 minutes. They will give off some liquid.

While the cucumbers are resting, in a large stainless steel or glass mixing bowl, stir together the chili flakes, garlic, grated apple, sugar, fish sauce, and ginger to form a paste.

Lift the cucumber pieces one at a time and brush the salt from them then add them to the paste. Use gloved hands to toss and coat the cucumbers evenly.

Add the green onions and carrot to the cucumbers in paste and toss to coat again.

Transfer the mixture to a clean glass container, like a quart (1 L) jar, and put a lid in place, but do not tighten it. Let this stand at room temperature for 12 to 18 hours before transferring to the refrigerator. Use within 7 days.

FRESH CUCUMBER *Relish*

It's bright. It's fresh. It's flavorful. It's vibrant. It's light. It's dead simple. Take your pick of any of those reasons to justify making this, but do make it. It's hard to beat a recipe that gives you so much for so little effort. Feel free to swap out the cilantro for the herb of your choice; parsley, chives, and mint are all delicious here. You can even double down on the onion and use the green portion of scallions in place of the herbs. Hit your crisper drawer and rustle up this fabulously fast side dish tonight and serve it with grilled, broiled, or fried fish or chicken.

YIELD: 6 SERVINGS

. . . .

INGREDIENTS

1 English (or seedless) cucumber, diced into ½-inch (13-mm) cubes (see Note)

1 sweet onion, peeled and diced into ¼–½-inch (6–13-mm) cubes

Juice of 1 lime

¼ cup (4 g) packed cilantro leaves, roughly chopped

2 tbsp (30 ml) garlic or regular olive oil

1 tsp kosher salt

½ tsp cracked black pepper

In a mixing bowl, toss together the cucumber, onion, lime juice, cilantro, garlic, salt, and pepper. This relish is best if allowed to meld and marry for at least 20 minutes in the refrigerator before serving, but it can be served immediately. For the best quality, eat within 48 hours.

NOTE

If you prefer your cucumber to be peeled, you can certainly peel it before dicing. I love cucumber peel, though, so I leave mine unpeeled.

Nana's Cucumbers IN YUMMY SAUCE

As a kid, I couldn't get enough of this oh-so simple, creamy salad of garden-fresh cucumbers and paper-thin sweet onions in homemade ranch dressing that was a dinner table fixture in the summer months. Whether my mom grew the cucumbers herself or bought them at the store, we all cheered when she served this up. It may sound ridiculously easy (because it is) but this retro recipe is a perfect match for grilled hamburgers, hot dogs, pork chops, chicken, and fish, and we also love it with roast chicken.

YIELD: 6 SERVINGS

. . . .

INGREDIENTS

1 cup (240 ml) sour cream

¼ cup (60 ml) milk

2 tbsp (12 g) Homemade Ranch Dressing Mix (page 256) or store-bought ranch dressing mix

2 tbsp (30 ml) fresh lemon juice

1 tbsp (3 g) finely chopped fresh dill or 1 tsp dill weed

1 tsp kosher salt

¼ tsp freshly ground black pepper

4 slicing cucumbers, cut into ¼-inch (6-mm) thick rounds (see Notes)

1 small sweet onion, peeled and sliced as thinly as possible

In a mixing bowl, whisk together the sour cream, milk, ranch dressing mix, lemon juice, dill, salt, and pepper. Toss in the cucumber and onion slices, cover the bowl tightly (or transfer to an airtight container), and refrigerate for at least 30 minutes before serving. Leftovers are good for up to 4 days. Stir well before serving leftovers.

NOTES

If your cucumbers have a tough skin, you might prefer to peel them before slicing. If it is a tender-skinned cucumber, the extra pop of green from leaving the skin on is quite pretty.

The sauce will thin the longer it is stored in the refrigerator. This is not a problem; it is just something to know ahead of time.

I like to save any leftover thin sauce. The cucumber and onion infuse the sauce nicely and it makes a tasty salad dressing.

CORN

Corn season is my favorite time of year. We have a couple of "nothing but the corn" dinners when fresh New York State corn is at its finest because fresh corn doesn't need to be anything but itself to be wonderful. Frozen corn, canned corn, and leftover sweet corn, however, can use a little bit of help in the star power department and I have you covered.

Modern Succotash (page 96) is a mainstay in our home all year long. Tender and crisp corn—whether canned, frozen, or cut from the cob—is stirred together with black beans, lime juice, garlic, onion, and a little fresh jalapeño for a lighter, fresher take on the classic succotash.

If you're looking for a sure-fire hit of a side dish to accompany fried chicken, chili, soups, or stews, try the Pepper Jack Corn Fritters (page 99), crispy, pan-fried, savory, melted cheese-studded corn cakes that can double as a vegetarian main dish.

And for all of your special occasions (and everyday occasions that could use a little special treatment) I present a Savory Corn Pudding (page 103). Serve this luscious, rich, and simple take on the Southern classic with roast turkey, chicken, pork, or beef for a meal no one will forget.

SHOPPING TIPS: Frozen corn is a no-brainer, but fresh corn requires a little more attention. You don't need to peel back husks to eyeball the kernels, though. Look for husks that are green, firm, tight, and not-dried-out.

Hold the ear in your hand and give it a gentle squeeze from top to bottom. It should feel heavy for its size, solid, and round with plump, plentiful kernels and no "empty" spaces which would indicate missing kernels.

Avoid husks with little brown holes which might indicate worms have taken up residence.

Finally, have a look at the tassels; they should be sticky and brown, not black and dry.

STORAGE: The good news is you can leave fresh corn at room temperature if you're going to cook it within a few hours. The bad news is that beyond that you want to store it in the crisper in your refrigerator and use it within one day of purchase. Oh, that delicious, ephemeral corn. Sigh.

MODERN *Succotash*

Is it a salsa? Is it a succotash? Is it a salad? Yes! It's all of these things and more importantly, it is one of my favorite all-purpose side dishes of all time owing to its deliciousness, versatility, and ease of preparation. Unlike traditional succotash, we sub in black beans for the lima beans and olive oil for the cream. It goes with absolutely everything from fish to flank steak and makes a mean tortilla chip dip, too. It's a no-cook dish, by nature, but you can heat it up if you fancy a warm version.

YIELD: 8 SERVINGS

. . . .

INGREDIENTS

1 (15-oz [425-g]) can black beans, drained and rinsed (see Notes)

1¾ cups (270 g) corn kernels (see Notes)

1 cup (130 g) halved cherry or grape tomatoes

½ sweet onion, diced

½ cup (8 g) fresh cilantro leaves or parsley, roughly chopped

2 cloves of garlic, minced or pressed in a garlic press

Juice of 2 limes

2 tbsp (30 ml) extra-virgin olive oil or Luke's Infused Garlic Oil (page 246)

¾ tsp kosher salt

In a medium mixing bowl, add the beans, corn, tomatoes, onion, cilantro, garlic, lime juice, oil, and salt and toss gently to combine. Serve immediately or refrigerate for up to 4 days.

NOTES

Swap in black eyed peas for the black beans to provide the tastiest and easiest nod to traditional Southern New Year's Day eating! This is the first bite we have every January 1st in our family.

For the corn, you can use kernels freshly cut from a raw or cooked ear of corn, frozen corn which has been thawed, or canned corn which has been drained. Dealer's choice!

PEPPER JACK *Corn Fritters*

Nothing, but nothing goes better with grilled foods in the summer or a pot of chili than these slightly spicy corn fritters bursting with the sweetness of corn, freshness of cilantro, green onion, jalapeño peppers, and loads of melted cheese. Be prepared for compliments when you make these!

YIELD: 8 SERVINGS

INGREDIENTS

6 green onions, trimmed of roots and thinly sliced, divided

3 cups (462 g) fresh corn kernels or canned or frozen corn (see Notes)

¼ cup (4 g) packed fresh cilantro leaves, roughly chopped

1 fresh jalapeño, seeds and stem removed, minced

Juice of ½ lime

1 cup (125 g) all-purpose flour (1-for-1 gluten-free flour can be used instead)

1 tsp baking powder

1 tsp chili powder

¾ tsp kosher salt

8 oz (226 g) shredded pepper Jack cheese

¼ cup (60 ml) milk

2 eggs, beaten

2–3 tbsp (30–45 ml) olive oil or sunflower oil, divided

Sea salt flakes, for garnish

Sour cream and salsa, for dipping, optional

Reserve 1 tablespoon (12 g) of the sliced green onions for garnish. In a large mixing bowl, combine the remaining green onions, corn, cilantro, jalapeño, and lime juice and toss to combine evenly.

In a separate small bowl, whisk together the flour, baking powder, chili powder, and salt, then toss that into the corn mixture and stir to combine. Add the cheese, milk, and eggs and stir until even.

Drizzle 1½ teaspoons (7 ml) of oil over the bottom of a 10- to 12-inch (25- to 30-cm) non-stick pan over medium-high heat. Scoop about ¼ cup (60 ml) of the corn fritter mixture into the pan and gently flatten with a heat-proof spatula. You can neaten up the edges, too, if you desire. Repeat until you have about 4 to 5 fritters in your pan. Fry for 2 to 3 minutes, or until you see golden brown edges. Slide a thin, flexible spatula under the fritter and carefully flip before frying for another 2 minutes. Transfer the fritters to a paper towel–lined plate and repeat the drizzle of oil and frying process until all of the mixture is cooked.

To keep the first batch of fritters crispy while making the second and third batches, place finished fritters in a single layer on a cooling rack over a cookie sheet in a 170°F (76°C) oven.

Serve the fritters garnished with sea salt and green onions with a side of sour cream and salsa.

NOTES

If you use canned corn, you'll need 2 (15-ounce [425-g]) cans that are well drained and patted dry with paper towels. Frozen corn can also be used, but will need to be thoroughly thawed and patted dry, too.

Leftovers can be stored in the refrigerator for up to 4 days and reheated in a single layer on a cookie sheet in a 350°F (176°C) oven just until hot all the way through, about 8 minutes, or they can be reheated in a frying pan with a smidgen of butter.

For a non-reactive saucepan, use stainless steel, non-stick, or glass. As long as it isn't aluminum, it will work.

GARDEN OF PLENTY *Salad*

This fabulously fresh salad is bursting with delicious garden goodies like snow peas, corn, cherry tomatoes, green onions, and a generous amount of fresh herbs all in a light, simple Mason Jar Vinaigrette (page 248) that's shaken together in seconds. It doesn't get much easier or fresher than this Garden of Plenty Salad. And while it's a natural to whip this up when your garden or CSA share is at peak production, you can easily make this from the grocery store in the winter months when you're craving something green and burstingly fresh! This is good for up to 4 days in the refrigerator, making it a great option for packing in your lunch!

YIELD: 8 SERVINGS

INGREDIENTS

1¾ cups (270 g) corn kernels (freshly cut from the cob, thawed from frozen, or drained from a can)

1¾ cups (261 g) cherry tomatoes, halved

1¾ cups (108 g) snow peas (or sugar snap peas)

6 green onions, trimmed and thinly sliced

⅓ cup (20 g) fresh parsley, roughly chopped

⅓ cup (10 g) fresh basil leaves, thinly sliced

⅓ cup (30 g) fresh mint, thinly sliced

2 tbsp (30 ml) Mason Jar Vinaigrette (page 248) or your favorite store-bought vinaigrette, plus more to serve

In a large mixing bowl, gently toss together the corn, tomatoes, snow peas, green onions, parsley, basil, and mint, until evenly distributed.

Drizzle 2 tablespoons (30 ml) of the vinaigrette over the salad and toss to coat. Refrigerate the salad or serve immediately with the additional vinaigrette at the table so you can add it to taste.

NOTE

Play around with the combination of herbs in this salad depending on what you have handy. It's also excellent with fresh cilantro and celery leaves.

SAVORY *Corn Pudding*

Bursting with corn, this cheesy, flavor-powerhouse casserole resembles a quiche more than it does a pudding, and it is delicious both in sweet corn season and in the fall with Thanksgiving Dinner and other cold-weather feasts. Whether you opt to use fresh-from-the-cob, frozen, or canned corn, you'll be blown away by this fabulous marriage of corn, cheese, and eggs. Psst, my daughter-in-law and I have made a full meal of this more than once.

YIELD: 8 SERVINGS

. . . .

INGREDIENTS

8 oz (226 g) of butter, melted, plus 2 tbsp (28 g) for the pan

2 cups (240 ml) whole milk

6 large eggs

3 tbsp (24 g) cornmeal

3 tbsp (24 g) all-purpose flour (1-for-1 gluten-free flour can be used here)

2 tsp (9 g) baking powder

1¼ tsp (10 g) kosher salt

¾ tsp granulated garlic

¾ tsp granulated onion

¾ tsp ground mustard powder

½ tsp ground black pepper

5 cups (770 g) of corn kernels, freshly cut from the cob (thawed from frozen, or well drained if canned)

12 oz (340 g) sharp Cheddar cheese, grated (about 3 cups)

1 green onion, thinly sliced

. . . .

SERVE WITH

Roasted, smoked, or deep-fried turkey, grilled or roast chicken, pork, or sausages.

Preheat the oven to 350°F (176°C) and grease a 9 x 13–inch (23 x 33–cm) casserole dish with the 2 tablespoons (28 g) of butter. Set it aside.

In a large mixing bowl, whisk together the melted butter, milk, and eggs. In a smaller bowl, use a fork or small whisk to combine the cornmeal, flour, baking powder, salt, granulated garlic and onion, mustard powder, and pepper until even in color. Whisk the flour mixture into the wet mixture, then use a spoon to stir in the corn kernels and Cheddar cheese. Transfer the mixture to the prepared baking dish and bake for 40 to 45 minutes, or until puffy, set in the center, and a knife inserted into the center of the casserole comes out clean.

Allow the casserole to set for 5 minutes, then garnish with sliced green onions and serve. Leftovers are delicious when stored in the refrigerator and reheated for up to 4 days after baking.

PEAS

Peas; once the grey-green, stodgy, canned stalwart of the American dinner table, they now have a new lease on life with the four gloriously green, magnificent side dishes here in this book.

Take this warning on our Bacon Pea Salad (page 106) seriously; when once you've brought this to a potluck or gathering, you'll be asked to bring it many, many more times. It's easy, though, so you'll be happy to oblige. Who wouldn't love a salad of poppingly fresh peas with a shocking amount of crispy bacon, shredded sharp Cheddar, and minced onion all in a creamy dressing that stirs together in one bowl?

Be prepared for oohs and aahs when you serve stunning Pea Hummus with Parsley Oil (page 110). It's a riot of green glory and it's fresher and lighter and more herbaceous than any hummus you've ever had before. And Pea, Pancetta, and Goat Cheese Pasta (page 109) comes together lickety-split with ingredients that are easy to find, and is an elegant, creamy side salad for grilled or roasted chicken and fish.

SHOPPING TIPS: Again, frozen peas are a no-brainer . . . they're one of the most perfect frozen foods ever. If, however, you find yourself in the presence of fresh peas, please select small to medium, bulging pods that are fresh looking and uncracked. It should be crisp and fresh enough to make a snapping sound when broken in half.

STORAGE: Fresh peas have a very short shelf-life and lose sweetness exponentially every day after harvest, so they're at their very, sweetest-best eaten, or blanched and frozen- within 2 days of being picked. Fresh peas in the pod can be stored for a day or two in the refrigerator, but to store longer, shell the peas and plop them into salted boiling water for just one minute before straining and chilling in a bowl of ice water. The peas should then be drained again, put into zip-top freezer bags, and frozen for up to 6 months.

BACON *Pea Salad*

The sweet pop of the pea, creamy mayonnaise dressing, crunchy mild red onion, and crispy bacon in this salad tastes great right after being stirred together, but even better after having a day long rest in the refrigerator. Serve this with any and all grilled meats, roast or fried chicken, or fried fish.

YIELD: 12 SERVINGS

. . . .

INGREDIENTS

1 lb (454 g) bacon cooked according to package instructions, drained of grease, and crumbled or finely chopped

2 lbs (907 g) shelled or frozen peas (see Notes)

¾ cup (85 g) coarsely grated Cheddar cheese

½ small red onion, peeled and finely chopped

½ cup (120 ml) mayonnaise

½ tsp kosher salt

½ tsp coarsely ground black pepper

¼ tsp paprika

Stir together the bacon, peas, cheese, onion, mayonnaise, salt, pepper, and paprika. Serve immediately, or (preferably) put the salad in a tightly-covered container in the refrigerator for at least 1 hour but up to 3 days before serving. Give the salad a gentle stir from top to bottom before serving.

NOTES

If using freshly shelled peas, you'll need to blanch them. To do this, bring a large pot of salted water to a rapid boil. Gently lower the peas into the water and boil for 1½ minutes. Immediately drain the peas and then transfer them to a bowl of ice water to stop cooking.

If using frozen peas, let them thaw in the refrigerator overnight or rapidly thaw them on the counter for 2 hours before using in the salad.

COLD VINAIGRETTE
Peas and Onions

Oh sure, this may not be the most exciting sounding dish, but this habit-forming, super refreshing, marinated pea and onion salad is just the thing for your next barbecue. Sweet and poppingly fresh peas, mild but flavorful pearl onions, fistfuls of fresh dill and parsley, and my favorite tangy Mason Jar Vinaigrette (page 248) combine to make a deliciously convenient salad that can be whipped up a day or two in advance. Serve with anything grilled, but it especially sings with fish dishes!

YIELD: 8 SERVINGS

INGREDIENTS

1 lb (454 g) frozen peas, thawed overnight (see Notes)

1 lb (454 g) frozen pearl onions, thawed overnight (see Notes)

⅓ cup (15 g) packed fresh dill leaves, roughly chopped

¼ cup (15 g) packed fresh parsley leaves, roughly chopped

¼ cup (60 ml) Mason Jar Vinaigrette (page 248)

1 tsp kosher salt

½ tsp freshly ground black pepper

In a mixing bowl, combine the peas, onions, dill, parsley, vinaigrette, salt, and pepper, and toss gently to coat. This salad can be served immediately but the flavor intensifies over time. Eat within 4 days of making for best taste.

NOTES

If you'd like to save a dish—and who wouldn't?—you can simply empty the frozen peas and pearl onions into a storage container with a tight-fitting lid, cover tightly, and let thaw in the refrigerator overnight. The next day, simply toss the chopped herbs, vinaigrette, salt, and pepper with the thawed peas and onions to coat.

If frozen pearl onions aren't your thing, or you have an abundance of fresh onions, feel free to sub in half a sweet onion, thinly sliced.

If you are swimming in fresh peas, blanch a pound (454 g) of them and shock in cold water, and they'll work perfectly in this salad!

BRUSSELS SPROUTS

Like many kids, I grew up thinking I didn't like Brussels sprouts. It turns out that what I didn't like was how I was eating them. Brussels sprouts have the most incredible crisp-tender texture when done right, and I love them enough to eat them a couple of times a week in the recipes included here.

Crispy Air-Fried Brussels Sprouts with a Sweet and Spicy Glaze (page 116) are my all-time favorite way to eat sprouts. Crispy, caramelized, salty outer leaves, tender insides, all tossed in a quick, tangy, chili pepper and honey glaze make these positively irresistible.

Whenever we have a festive meal or a special occasion, we bring out our Roasted Brussels Sprouts with Grapes and Walnuts (page 119). While it may sound like an odd combination, it's perfect—trust me.

And Brussels Sprouts with Kielbasa (page 123) made my husband a very happy man. Once again, we're roasting the sprouts to bring out the sweetness and it matches perfectly with tiny flavorful crisped morsels of garlicky kielbasa. It's a match made in heaven for roasts of all sorts.

SHOPPING TIPS: Fresh Brussels sprouts are most commonly sold in one of three ways; on the stalk, in pre-measured bags by weight, or loose in a bulk bin. If you're not sure how soon you'll use them, I recommend buying them on the stalk if at all possible. Any which way, the sweetest, freshest sprouts are small, firm, and a bright, uniform green with compact, tight leaves.

STORAGE: If you buy Brussels sprouts on the stalk, store them on the stalk in the refrigerator, with the end in a jar of water or wrapped in a plastic bag in the crisper drawer for optimal freshness.

To store sprouts that were already cut from the stalk, put them in a sealed plastic bag in the crisper drawer of your refrigerator.

While Brussels sprouts are sweetest when they're freshest, you can plan on Brussels sprouts off the stalk staying good for about 1 week when stored as discussed above and sprouts on the stalk giving you about 10 days.

Note: Brussels sprouts are ethylene sensitive.

CRISPY AIR-FRIED *Brussels Sprouts* WITH A SWEET AND SPICY GLAZE

I am 100% obsessed with these crispy-leaved, deeply caramelized Brussels sprouts with tender insides that are "fried" in an air-fryer. If you don't have an air-fryer, don't worry! I've included instructions on how to get a similar result from the oven in the Note section. The chili pepper in the recipe is optional, but a little hit of heat takes this recipe to the next level!

YIELD: 5 SERVINGS

INGREDIENTS

1½ lbs (680 g) small Brussels sprouts, quartered

2 tbsp (30 ml) Luke's Infused Garlic Oil (page 246) or sunflower or canola oil

1 red Fresno or jalapeño pepper, stem removed, thinly sliced, optional

½ tsp kosher salt, plus more to taste

¼ cup (60 ml) mild honey

2 tbsp (30 ml) fresh lime juice or rice vinegar

1 tsp Sriracha, optional, or 1 additional tsp of lime juice or vinegar

SERVE WITH

Burgers, roast chicken or turkey, or pork chops

Preheat your air-fryer to 390°(199°C) for at least 5 minutes. When it reaches the proper temperature, toss the quartered Brussels sprouts and oil in a bowl then pour into the air fryer pan. Reserve the bowl.

Air fry for 18 minutes. At the 9-minute mark, shake the pan and add in the pepper slices, if using, and salt, and continue cooking for the remaining time or until the Brussels sprouts are crispy and well-browned.

While the sprouts are frying, whisk the honey, lime juice, and Sriracha together in the bowl you tossed the sprouts in with the oil. Add the hot Brussels sprouts and peppers to the bowl and toss to coat. Serve immediately.

NOTE

To prepare these in an oven, place a rimmed, metal half-sheet pan on a rack situated in the upper third of the oven and preheat to 475°F (246°C). When the oven reaches the correct temperature, prepare the sprouts with oil as directed above and add to the hot sheet pan. Return the pan to the oven and roast for 20 minutes. Remove the pan from the oven and use a metal or heat proof spatula to slide underneath the sprouts and flip them over or at least stir them. Toss the slices of pepper over the sprouts, if using, and add the salt. Return the pan once again to the oven and roast for another 8 minutes. Toss with the honey, lime, and Sriracha mixture. Serve immediately.

Roasted Brussels Sprouts
WITH GRAPES AND WALNUTS

I know you probably have never thought, "Gosh, I need to roast some Brussels sprouts with grapes and walnuts . . ." but stick with me here; this is a life changing recipe and you certainly will think that often after you try this. When tossed with olive oil and popped in the oven to roast, Brussels sprouts become crisp-edged and crazy tender inside, grapes become caramelized and extra-juicy, and walnuts? Well, shoot. They're toasty and fragrant when roasted alongside the sprouts and grapes. While the pan is still sizzling hot, you hit it with a little balsamic vinegar to push this dish into pure-heaven territory. Even better, it's all made on one pan and it's super easy! Serve this with pork, chicken, turkey, lamb, or beef prepared any which way.

YIELD: 8 SERVINGS

INGREDIENTS

1½ lbs (680 g) fresh Brussels sprouts, stem ends trimmed and cut in half or quartered, depending upon size

1½ lbs (680 g) red or black seedless grapes, removed from the stems

3 tbsp (45 ml) olive oil

½ tsp coarse kosher salt

½ tsp freshly ground black pepper

½ cup (55 g) shelled walnut halves and large pieces

2 tbsp (30 ml) balsamic vinegar

1 tsp coarse Maldon sea salt flakes

Preheat the oven to 400°F (204°C). Pile the Brussels sprouts and grapes onto a rimmed half-sheet pan. Drizzle the olive oil over the sprouts and grapes, sprinkle with the kosher salt and pepper, and toss to coat. Shake the pan to distribute the sprouts and grapes evenly over the surface. It should be a single layer. Roast for 10 minutes before scattering the walnuts over the sprouts. Return the pan to the oven and roast for another 10 to 15 minutes or until the sprouts are tender and caramelized and the grapes are shiny and fat.

As soon as you get the pan out of the oven, drizzle the balsamic vinegar over the top. It should sizzle. Toss to distribute, transfer to a serving dish, and scatter the sea salt flakes over the top.

NOTES

Leftovers are incredible reheated for breakfast and served with a frizzled, fried, or poached egg.

Maldon sea salt flakes are large, thin, uneven, crunchy, clean-tasting salt flakes meant for finishing food. If you cannot find this, you can substitute other sea salt flakes, but do so to taste.

SHAVED *Brussels Sprouts Salad* WITH BACON AND DRIED CHERRIES

This salad of crisp-tender Brussels sprouts with tart, sweet dried cherries, green onions, and a warm bacon vinaigrette is going to be your new go-to salad for pork roasts or roast chicken. It's amazing right after it's made when it's still slightly warm, but it's equally wonderful after being stashed in the refrigerator for a couple of days. Pack leftovers in your lunch and you'll be one very happy camper.

YIELD: 12 SERVINGS

INGREDIENTS

½ lb (226 g) bacon

2 lbs (907 g) fresh Brussels sprouts, halved or quartered if they're large

1½ tsp (9 g) kosher salt, divided

1 cup (150 g) dried cherries

1 bunch green onions, thinly sliced

¼ cup (60 ml) apple cider vinegar

2 tbsp (28 g) raw sugar or brown sugar

2 tbsp (30 ml) water

¾ tsp freshly ground black pepper

Preheat the oven to 400°F (204°C). Line a half-sheet pan with heavy-duty aluminum foil. Arrange the bacon on the foil. Bake for 12 to 20 minutes, depending on the thickness of the bacon and the crispiness you desire. Immediately transfer the crisped bacon to a paper towel–lined plate and then carefully use the foil to pour 3 tablespoons (45 ml) of the bacon fat into a measuring cup. Set the bacon drippings aside. Chop the bacon and set aside.

Fit a food processor with a thin slicing blade. Drop the Brussels sprouts into the feed chute, shaving all of the sprouts. Transfer the shaved sprouts to a mixing bowl. Sprinkle ½ teaspoon of the salt over the sprouts and toss with your hands. Scatter the cherries, green onions, and bacon over the shaved sprouts and set aside.

In a non-reactive saucepan placed over medium-high heat, combine the reserved bacon fat, vinegar, sugar, water, remaining teaspoon of salt, and pepper. Bring the sauce to a boil and whisk to combine, then immediately pour over the contents of the mixing bowl. Toss to coat. This salad can be served immediately or stored in an airtight container in the refrigerator for up to 3 days.

NOTES

To change things up from time to time, swap in dried cranberries for the dried cherries. Either way it's sublime!

For a non-reactive saucepan, use stainless steel, non-stick or glass. As long as it isn't aluminum, it will work.

Brussels Sprouts WITH KIELBASA

If Brussels sprouts look like bite-size cabbages, and cabbage is often served with kielbasa, then it stands to reason that it should be served with bite-size kielbasa . . . or at least that seems logical to me! Any way you look at it, the sweet, tender Brussels sprouts match perfectly with crispy-edged, rich, garlicky little cubes of kielbasa. Best of all, this is the ultimate in low-maintenance side dishes as it all comes together on one sheet pan in the oven. Serve this with pork, chicken, or beef prepared any which way.

YIELD: 8 SERVINGS

INGREDIENTS

1½ lbs (680 g) fresh Brussels sprouts, stem ends trimmed and halved or quartered

6 oz (170 g) kielbasa or smoked sausage, diced in ½-inch (1.3-cm) cubes

2 tbsp (30 ml) olive oil

½ tsp coarse kosher salt

½ tsp freshly ground black pepper

2 tbsp (30 ml) red wine vinegar

½ tsp coarse Maldon sea salt flakes (see Notes)

Preheat the oven to 425°F (220°C). Pile the Brussels sprouts and kielbasa onto a rimmed half-sheet pan. Drizzle the olive oil over, sprinkle with the salt and pepper, and toss to coat. Shake the pan to distribute the sprouts and sausage evenly over the surface. It should be a single layer. Roast for 10 minutes before giving the pan a good shake to move things around or using a spatula to flip and stir. Return the pan to the oven and roast for another 10 to 15 minutes or until the sprouts are tender and caramelized and the kielbasa is well browned and crisp at the edges.

As soon as you get the pan out of the oven, drizzle the vinegar over the top. It should sizzle. Toss to distribute, transfer to a serving dish, and scatter the sea salt over the top.

NOTES

Much like my Roasted Brussels Sprouts with Grapes and Walnuts (page 119) leftovers of this dish make an incredible breakfast or brunch when reheated and topped with a fried egg and accompanied by toast.

Maldon sea salt flakes are large, thin, uneven, crunchy, clean-tasting salt flakes meant for finishing food. If you cannot find this, you can substitute other sea salt flakes, but do so to taste.

ASPARAGUS

Ah, asparagus. The first sign that spring is finally springing near me is the appearance of "Asparagus for sale. U-cut" signs on roadsides and boy does that spark joy!

Perfect asparagus doesn't require much to be done to it to make it delicious, but it does require some specific handling to get the best result. Try my Garlicky Baked Asparagus Fries (page 126) for a handheld, crunchy-coated, eminently snackable treatment outside of your everyday asparagus world.

And for the most excellent, far-from-basic, but simplest roasted asparagus of all time, look to our Lemon-Pepper Roasted Asparagus (page 129); a gently citrusy and peppery tender asparagus with all the concentrated, fragrant goodness that roasting the spears can give.

Before you cook your asparagus, you should remove any dry ends. The easiest way to remove woody ends from the asparagus spears is by holding each end and bending until it snaps. It will naturally snap off where the ends become tough.

SHOPPING TIPS: Look for bundles of plump, firm spears of a uniform size and color with tightly closed tips. Try to avoid spears that are rubbery or ones that become very pale or woody a couple of inches from the bottom of the stalks.

STORAGE: When you get your asparagus home, keep them bundled with the rubber band (or bundle them with a rubber band or piece of kitchen twine). Trim an inch (2.5 cm) off of the ends of the spears and put them into a jar or cup with 2 inches (5 cm) of water in the bottom. Cover the asparagus and jar loosely with a bag or drape with plastic wrap but do not close the bag or cinch the wrap. Store the asparagus in the refrigerator for up to a week, changing the water if it begins to look cloudy.

GARLICKY BAKED *Asparagus Fries*

I'm a sucker for any vegetable dish you eat with your hands and this crunchy-coated, tender roasted asparagus is definitely one of the things I attack and eat with no mercy. Whether dipped in our excellent Smoked Paprika Chipotle Sauce (page 252), in Garlic Buffalo Wing Sauce (page 255), or in a beautiful lemon aioli, these asparagus fries will disappear—no magic needed. This is excellent with roasted or grilled chicken or pork or pan-fried fish.

YIELD: 8 SERVINGS

INGREDIENTS

¾ cup (42 g) unseasoned panko bread crumbs, divided

½ cup (63 g) all-purpose flour (1-for-1 gluten-free flour can be used instead)

½ cup (120 ml) water

1 tsp Montreal steak seasoning

½ tsp granulated garlic

1 lb (454 g) bunch asparagus, preferably medium-sized stalks, trimmed of woody ends

Thinly-sliced green onions or parsley, for garnish

Smoked Paprika Chipotle Sauce (page 252), or dip of your choice, for serving.

Preheat the oven to 450°F (232°C). Line a baking sheet with heavy-duty foil, dull side up, spray with non-stick cooking spray or brush with oil, and sprinkle ¼ cup (14 g) of the panko crumbs over the pan, then set aside.

In a large mixing bowl, whisk together the flour, water, steak seasoning, and garlic until smooth. Add the asparagus spears into the bowl and gently toss to coat thoroughly. Use tongs to transfer the asparagus to the prepared pan and place them on top of the panko crumbs. Scatter the remaining ½ cup (28 g) of panko crumbs over the spears and use the tongs to toss to coat them in the crumbs. Spread the spears out so there is some space for air to circulate around them in the oven.

Bake for 25 minutes, or until the coating is set and the crumbs are golden brown in places. Let the asparagus rest on the pan for 3 minutes, then use a thin, flexible spatula to transfer the spears to a serving dish. Garnish with green onions or parsley and serve with dip.

LEMON-PEPPER *Roasted Asparagus*

When you add a little bright lemon and black pepper and just a hint of roasted garlic to the natural sweetness of roasted asparagus, you end up with a side dish that is a beautiful match to grilled, baked, or broiled fish, chicken, and lamb. It doesn't get much easier than this, but wow is it ever good.

YIELD: 6 SERVINGS

INGREDIENTS

1 lb (454 g) thin asparagus spears (see Notes)

3 tbsp (45 ml) olive oil

¾ tsp kosher salt

¾ tsp freshly ground black pepper

1 clove of garlic, peeled and minced

1 tbsp (15 ml) freshly squeezed lemon juice

1 tsp fresh lemon zest

Preheat the oven to 425°F (220°C). Pile the asparagus spears on a rimmed half-sheet pan. Drizzle with the olive oil and use your hands or tongs to toss them to coat, then distribute them over the pan in a single layer. Sprinkle with the salt, pepper, and garlic.

Roast for 12 to 15 minutes, or until the asparagus is tender and caramelized a bit at the tips. When you take the pan from the oven, quickly sprinkle the lemon juice and lemon zest over the asparagus and toss to coat. Serve immediately.

NOTES

You can make this with thicker asparagus spears, but it may take a few more minutes for the asparagus to roast to tenderness.

If you prefer plain, roasted asparagus, just omit the lemon juice and lemon zest! This is still the most perfect way to roast asparagus.

CREAMY PARMESAN
Asparagus Bake

One glimpse of a casserole dish filled with tender asparagus baked in bubbling, creamy Parmesan sauce is going to set your appetite raging, so you might want to make sure your main dish is ready to go! Pair this simple and savory treatment of spring's favorite harbinger with roast lamb, chicken, or beef.

YIELD: 4 SERVINGS

INGREDIENTS

1 tbsp (14 g) butter, softened

1 lb (454 g) asparagus, trimmed of dry ends, cut into 2-inch (5-cm) pieces, about 4 cups of cut asparagus

1 cup (240 ml) heavy cream

½ cup (50 g) freshly-grated Parmesan cheese

1 clove of garlic, peeled and minced

1 tsp kosher salt

Preheat the oven to 350°F (176°C). Butter a 1- to 2-quart (1- to 2-L) baking dish or an 8 x 8-inch (20 x 20-cm) square baking pan.

Scatter the asparagus into the buttered dish. In a small mixing bowl, gently stir together the cream, cheese, garlic, and salt. Pour over the asparagus. Bake for 20 minutes, or until the sauce is bubbly and golden brown on top and the asparagus is tender when pierced with a sharp knife.

EGGPLANT

The recipes I'm sharing here with you I love to the point where I can eat myself sick on them. And I usually don't dig eggplant. It's true. So please, if you think you don't like eggplant, give these a try. You may surprise even yourself!

The Easiest, Most Ultimate Baba Ghanoush (page 134) is a fluffy, garlicky, silky smooth puree of roasted eggplant that helped convert me from an eggplant refuser to someone willing to try all eggplant dishes. You can serve it alongside all Mediterranean main dishes, grilled chicken, and fish, but it is also great as a stand-alone dip for warm pita bread, roasted vegetables, or raw veggie sticks.

And when it comes to the *ne plus ultra* of eggplant, all credit goes to my husband who decided to use up a couple of eggplants one day while frying chicken and created Chicken-Fried Eggplant (page 137). My word, but this is good stuff. And hey-o! While it makes a side dish worthy of your best Southern-fried chicken, of course, it also makes a crazy-good vegetarian main dish!

Eggplants are found in many different varieties, but the most commonly available types are the globe (the classic large, oblong aubergine with deep-purple skin), the Italian (similar to the globe, but slightly smaller), and Japanese eggplant which is longer and narrower. They can all be used for any of the recipes in this book.

SHOPPING TIPS: Look for an eggplant with smooth, shiny skin and deep color and that is heavy for its size. A ripe eggplant should be firm but not hard. To test for ripeness, gently press a finger against the skin. If it leaves a mark, it is ripe. If it feels very soft or you're able to puncture the skin, it is over ripe and should be avoided.

The stem end of the eggplant should be green and free of mold or mushiness.

STORAGE: Eggplant is best stored in a cool spot away from direct light and eaten within 2 days of purchase. You can squeak out 3 more days if you store it in the crisper drawer of the refrigerator, but avoid sealing them in plastic bags which would accelerate decay.

Note: Eggplants are extremely ethylene sensitive.

THE EASIEST, MOST ULTIMATE
Baba Ghanoush

Silky smooth, slightly smoky, creamy, fluffy, and garlicky eggplant dip is totally crave-worthy, but first, let's get this out of the way; Baba Ghanoush is one of the most fun recipe names ever to say out loud. Try it a few times. I'll wait . . . Not at all coincidentally, it's one of the most fun to eat! It gets a reputation for being finicky and difficult to make, but this version is both the tastiest I've ever had and the easiest to make.

YIELD: 4 SERVINGS

INGREDIENTS

1 large eggplant or 2 small to medium eggplants, cut in half lengthwise

⅓ cup (80 ml) extra-virgin olive oil or Luke's Infused Garlic Oil (page 246), divided, plus 1 tbsp (15 ml) for garnish

2½ tbsp (37 g) tahini

2 cloves of garlic, peeled and minced

2 tbsp (30 ml) lemon juice

1 tsp kosher salt

2 tbsp (8 g) roughly-chopped fresh parsley, for garnish

1 green onion, thinly sliced, for garnish

Pita chips, pita bread, naan, or raw vegetables, for serving

SERVE WITH

Mediterranean-spiced grilled chicken, lamb, or fish

Preheat the oven to 425°F (220°C). Brush the cut sides of the eggplants with 1 teaspoon of the oil each. Brush a half-sheet pan or other rimmed baking sheet with 1 tablespoon (15 ml) of the olive oil. Place the eggplant halves, cut side down, on the baking sheet. Cut 2 lengthwise slits through the skin of each eggplant and brush with 1 tablespoon (15 ml) of olive oil.

Roast for 30 to 40 minutes, or until the eggplants are quite soft all the way through. Remove the eggplant halves from the oven and let them rest until they are cool enough to comfortably handle. Scoop the flesh into a colander and let it drain for 5 minutes. Discard the skin.

Transfer the eggplant flesh to a food processor with the rest of the olive oil, tahini, garlic, lemon juice, and salt, and blend until silky smooth and creamy.

You can serve this immediately, or store in the refrigerator, tightly covered, for up to a week. Garnish before serving with a drizzle of olive oil (about 1 tablespoon [15 ml]), chopped parsley, and green onion. Serve with pita chips, warm pita bread or naan, or raw vegetables for dipping.

CHICKEN-FRIED *Eggplant*

I love Chicken-Fried Eggplant truly, madly, and deeply. This dish came about when we were making fried chicken and two giant eggplant were perched in our CSA share. My husband decided to treat it like the fried chicken, and moments later we were all, and I do mean all, scarfing down the crunchy coated, super tender and juicy, bite-size pieces of eggplant. And even better, I no longer flinched every time I saw "3 pounds (1.4 kg) of eggplant" on the grab list at my CSA.

YIELD: 4 SERVINGS

. . . .

INGREDIENTS

6 cups (1.4 L) sunflower, canola, or vegetable oil for frying (see Note)

2 cups (250 g) all-purpose flour

1 tsp kosher salt, plus more for serving

1 tsp fresh, coarse-ground black pepper

½ tsp paprika

½ tsp granulated garlic

½ tsp granulated onion

1 egg

1 cup (240 ml) buttermilk

1 large eggplant, peeled and cut into bite-size pieces

. . . .

SERVE WITH

Fried chicken, pork chops, or as a vegetarian main dish

Pour the oil into a large, deep, heavy-bottomed pan (or deep fryer) over medium to medium-high heat, adjusting as necessary to reach 375°F (190°C). If you have a deep fryer, set the temperature at 375°F. Remember not to fill your pan more than halfway full of oil.

In a mixing bowl, whisk together the flour, salt, pepper, paprika, granulated garlic, and granulated onion. Divide the flour between two pie plates and set aside.

Add the egg and buttermilk to a mixing bowl and whisk to combine thoroughly. Arrange one plate of flour on either side of the buttermilk mixture. Working with one piece of eggplant at a time, drag it through the first bowl of flour, shaking off the excess. Next, dip the eggplant in the buttermilk mixture, lifting and letting the excess drain away, then dip in the second plate of flour, turning it to coat it well.

Now carefully lower the eggplant into the oil. Repeat until all of the eggplant is frying, dividing it into more than one batch if needed to avoid overcrowding the pan. Stir the eggplant gently with tongs and allow to cook for about 8 minutes, or until the coating is beautifully golden brown and crisp. Transfer the hot eggplant to a paper towel–lined plate. Sprinkle with additional salt, if desired, before serving.

NOTE

When the oil you've used has cooled, you can pour it through a strainer into a jar with a tight-fitting lid and store in the refrigerator to reuse for deep frying again.

THYME-ROASTED *Eggplant*

Are you a fan of the silky texture of eggplant when it's done right? You can choose to roast it in an oven or on the grill for a little smokiness, but either way, you'll flip over how easy velvety, flavorful eggplant is to make to accompany roast or grilled lamb or beef. Served right in the skin to be scooped with a spoon, this eggplant is soft, delicious, and deeply caramel brown.

YIELD: 2 GENEROUS SERVINGS

INGREDIENTS

2 lbs (907 g) eggplant, halved lengthwise (2-4 eggplants depending on the variety)

1½ tsp (9 g) kosher salt

3 tbsp (45 ml) Luke's Infused Garlic Oil (page 246) or extra-virgin olive oil

10 sprigs of fresh thyme, divided

Lemon wedges, optional, for serving

Soft goat cheese, optional, for serving

Use the tip of a sharp knife to deeply score into the eggplant in a diamond pattern. To do this, score 2 or 3 long slices from the left downward to the right at an angle, then do the same thing from the right downward to the left at the same degree of angle.

Use your fingers to open the cuts of the eggplant and sprinkle the salt evenly over the halves. Leave these, cut side up, on the cutting board for 30 minutes.

Preheat oven to 400°F (204°C).

Flip the eggplant over the sink and squeeze to remove the salty liquid. Pat the eggplant thoroughly dry with paper towels, then place them, cut side up, on a rimmed half-sheet pan. Brush the cut sides thoroughly with all of the oil. Flip each half of the eggplant cut side down onto 4 sprigs of thyme on the pan.

Roast for 1 hour, or until the eggplant has collapsed in shape and is a deep brown color. Let the eggplant cool for 20 minutes before using a broad, sturdy metal spatula to flip them gently onto a serving dish. Strip the thyme leaves from the remaining sprigs and sprinkle evenly over the eggplant halves. Serve the halves with a lemon wedge and a slice of soft goat cheese, if desired.

MUSHROOMS

To say I love mushrooms is the understatement of the century. I'll take them any which way you serve them, but I do have some favorites and they are included here!

Oven-"Seared" Mushrooms (page 142) aren't actually seared, but they taste like they are! The method to our tasty madness is a super-high roast that creates the same flavor-concentrated, caramelized edges that we mushroom lovers covet so much.

Since I was using the oven to "sear" mushrooms, I figured I'd try my hand at using the oven to "fry" mushrooms and was thrilled with the result. Oven-"Fried" Breaded Mushrooms (page 146) are crunchy, umami-packed, and just waiting to be dunked in Smoked Paprika Chipotle Sauce (page 252) or marinara sauce. If you happen to own an air-fryer, I've also included instructions on how to use that for this recipe.

Important Note: While it may be tempting to wash the dirt off of mushrooms, it's the wrong move. Mushrooms are like sponges and love to soak up moisture. Keep a toothbrush dedicated to the job and gently brush the dirt off. If your mushrooms are fresh, this should be pretty easy to do.

SHOPPING TIPS: Whether buying loose or pre-packaged mushrooms, look for tightly-closed caps that are firm and evenly colored with a fresh, smooth appearance and no soft or wet spots. Tightly closed gills will indicate a more delicate flavor while open ones will indicate a more robust flavor.

STORAGE: Store mushrooms in a paper bag or a paper towel–lined and covered colander in the refrigerator. Wild varieties of mushrooms will last for up to 5 days while cultivated mushrooms will last for 1 to 2 weeks stored this way.

Mushrooms are like scent sponges, so avoid storing them next to pungent smelling foods.

Note: Mushrooms are ethylene sensitive.

OVEN-"SEARED" *Mushrooms*

Seared mushrooms are one of my all-time favorite side dishes because they go with so many things but sometimes I don't feel like standing in front of the stove adding mushrooms to a pan in batches and stirring. Enter oven "searing": stage left. It turns out that you can get the same crispy-brown edges and caramelized surfaces that searing yields by using the same "hot pan" method that we use for our Roasted Ginger-Sesame Green Beans (page 172) and our Spicy Asian Roasted Broccoli (page 32). Glory, hallelujah! Hit it with fresh herbs at the end if you'd like, but it's not obligatory. Serve with roast or grilled beef, pork, or chicken.

YIELD: 6 SERVINGS

· ·

INGREDIENTS

1½ lbs (680 g) baby portabella or white button mushrooms, sliced (see Note)

3 tbsp (45 ml) Luke's Infused Garlic Oil (page 246) or regular olive oil

¾ tsp kosher salt

½ tsp cracked or ground black pepper

Fresh thyme or torn parsley leaves, for garnish, optional

Place a rimmed, metal half-sheet pan on a rack situated in the upper third of the oven and preheat the oven to 475°F (246°C).

When the oven reaches the proper temperature, toss the mushrooms, oil, salt, and pepper together, and then pour onto the hot pan, using a spoon or spatula to distribute the mushrooms evenly over the surface. It should be sizzling.

Return the pan to the oven and roast for 15 minutes. Remove the pan from the oven and use a metal or heat-proof spatula to slide underneath the mushrooms and flip them over or at least stir them. Return the pan once again to the oven and roast for another 5 minutes. Sprinkle the mushrooms with fresh herbs, if desired. These are best served hot or warm.

NOTE

Do not wash your mushrooms before using this method. If they have dirt on them, brush off with a paper towel or toothbrush dedicated to the job. Using water to remove the dirt will waterlog the mushrooms and render them incapable of being seared; you'll end up with steamed mushrooms instead.

MAGICAL *Marinated Beets*

Beets: If you love them, then you LOVE them. And you're probably sorely tempted by those $5 boxes of about 4 or 5 tiny marinated beets in the produce section. Step away, though, friends, because you can make three times as many beets that are infinitely more delicious for the same price at home. Even better, you can customize them to use what you have on hand and what you love best. These marinated beets are fabulous with burgers, ham, and sandwiches. You could even make an Australian style hamburger by putting a big slice of marinated beet on top of your burger patty. Your salads, dinners, and lunches just got upgraded!

YIELD: 6 SERVINGS

INGREDIENTS

3 cups (250–300 g) sliced, cubed, or wedge-cut Simple Roasted Beets (page 150)

½ cup (120 ml) Mason Jar Vinaigrette (page 248) (made with the leftover beet oil, if desired!)

¼ cup (15 g) minced fresh parsley (chives, green onions, or cilantro also work here)

½ tsp kosher salt

½ tsp freshly ground black pepper

Combine the beets, vinaigrette, parsley, salt, and pepper in a container with an airtight lid, fix the lid in place, and gently turn the container upside down and right side up 3 to 4 times. Let the beets rest in the refrigerator for at least 30 minutes, but up to a week. Flip the container over 2 to 3 times before opening to serve.

NOTE

Save the accumulated vinaigrette and juices from the container when you're done with the beets. It makes a wonderful salad dressing for spinach salads. A tablespoon or two (15 or 30 ml) of it is also lovely in beef vegetable soup.

RIDICULOUSLY EASY HERBED BEET AND GOAT CHEESE *Salad*

Sometimes you just need to impress somebody, even if that somebody is you, and this is just the salad to do that. It's pretty flexible, too. You can start with Simple Roasted Beets (page 150) or Magical Marinated Beets (page 153); whichever you have on hand. You can use whichever fresh herbs you have that you love. Plain goat cheese is divine on here, but you can also use any herbed or fruit crusted variety, and if you're out of goat cheese, Boursin-style cheese and feta work great, too! Serve this with roast chicken or lamb.

YIELD: 4 SERVINGS

INGREDIENTS

2 cups (200 g) Magical Marinated Beets (page 153), drained with dressing reserved

3 oz (85 g) goat cheese, crumbled

¼ cup (15 g) minced fresh herbs (see Note)

1 tbsp (15 ml) extra-virgin olive oil

¼ tsp freshly ground black pepper

Arrange the beets in a serving dish and drizzle with 1 tablespoon (15 ml) of the reserved dressing. Scatter the goat cheese and fresh herbs over the top. Drizzle the olive oil over the top and sprinkle the pepper over the works. Serve immediately.

NOTE

My favorite combination for this salad is parsley, chives, green onions, and sometimes mint. Use whichever fresh herbs you have on hand in whichever combination you love best. The exceptions to this rule are fresh rosemary, oregano, tarragon, and thyme, which are far stronger in flavor. If using rosemary or oregano, use no more than ½ teaspoon of the leaves, very finely chopped. If using fresh tarragon or thyme, you can use 1 teaspoon of minced tarragon leaves or whole thyme leaves. I still recommend adding more parsley to the party, but you don't want the strong herbs to overwhelm every other flavor in the dish.

BEET AND WHITE BEAN *Hummus*

This showstopping, ultra-smooth, white bean puree is definitely not your traditional hummus; it's surprisingly subtle in flavor even though it is such an in-your-face hot pink. Roasted beets, cannellini beans, fresh lemon juice and zest, roasted garlic, and crumbled feta are pureed together to form this gorgeous, sophisticated, magenta twist on the well-known spread. This is excellent anywhere you'd nibble hummus, from using as a dip for raw veggies or pita wedges to spreading on sandwiches, and even tossing with hot pasta as a gorgeous pasta sauce. This is made to impress your taste buds and your eyes! Serve this hummus with hamburgers, grilled sausages, or roast turkey, chicken, or lamb.

YIELD: 6 SERVINGS (2 CUPS [480 ML])

INGREDIENTS

1 serving (1–2 beets) of Simple Roasted Beets (page 150)

1 (15-oz [425-g]) can of cannellini beans, drained and rinsed

1 lemon, zested and juiced

2 cloves of roasted garlic, squeezed from their papery peel (see Notes)

1 cup (150 g) crumbled feta

½ tsp kosher salt

½ tsp freshly ground black pepper

¼ cup (60 ml) extra-virgin olive oil

Add the beets, beans, lemon zest and juice, garlic, cheese, salt, and pepper to a food processor fitted with a metal blade. Process for 2 minutes, stopping occasionally to scrape down the sides of the bowl. With the food processor still running, drizzle in the olive oil and continue processing until perfectly smooth and silky, about 2 minutes more. This stores well, tightly covered, in the refrigerator for up to a week.

NOTES

To use this as pasta sauce, toss 1 to 1½ cups (240–360 ml) of the beet hummus with freshly boiled, drained pasta, thinning with the pasta water, 1 tablespoon (15 ml) at a time, to help coat the pasta.

Refer to the recipe for Whipped Feta–Stuffed Cherry Tomatoes (page 65) for instructions on how to roast garlic.

BODACIOUS *Beet Greens* WITH BACON

Beet greens are one of my husband's favorite foods, and this is his most-loved version. We both love the flavorful, tangy, bacon-rich, umami-filled, ruby-red potlikker that you can only get from using both the beet stems and greens. Whether we serve this with fried, roasted, or grilled chicken or pork, we're especially fond of having some fresh cornbread with it for soaking up all those delicious juices.

YIELD: 8 SERVINGS

INGREDIENTS

2 lbs (907 g) beet greens and stems (discard any especially thick or woody stems)

4 slices thick-cut bacon, cut into ¼-inch (6-mm) strips

1 yellow onion, peeled and diced

¾ tsp kosher salt

3 cloves of garlic, peeled and thinly sliced

¼ –½ tsp crushed red pepper flakes, depending on your heat preference

¾ cup (180 ml) water

1 tbsp (15 g) sugar or (15 ml) honey

3 tbsp (45 ml) apple cider or red wine vinegar

Wash the beet greens and stems in a sink full of fresh, cold water. Be sure to swish the greens around in the water. Fish the greens and stems from the sink and rinse them a second time in a colander. Pull the greens away from the stems. Cut them into bite-size pieces and put them in the colander. Dice the stems the same size as you diced the onion. Set aside.

Place the bacon strips in a 12-inch (30-cm) skillet over medium heat. Stir and cook until the bacon is crisp, then use a slotted spoon to transfer the bacon to a paper towel–lined plate.

Return the pan with the bacon fat to medium heat and add the onion, beet stems, and salt. Cook, stirring occasionally, for 5 to 7 minutes, or until the onion and beet stems start to soften. Stir in the garlic and red pepper flakes and cook for 1 more minute before adding the water and sugar. Stir, scraping the bottom of the pan to loosen up any deliciousness that may be stuck. Bring the mixture to a boil, add the beet greens, cover the pan and reduce the heat to low, simmering until the greens are tender, about 5 to 10 minutes. If your greens are quite mature, it may be closer to 15 minutes.

Drizzle the vinegar over the greens, toss in the bacon and serve hot or warm.

NOTE

Leftover beet greens and their potlikker are delicious added to ham and/or bean soups. Be aware that the red color of the potlikker will definitely make itself known in large amounts, though.

BELL PEPPERS

Bell peppers are everywhere! That's a good thing, though, because they're desirable and you want to have them around all of the time because they deliver major color and flavor with minimal work. And here's a fun fact for you. All colors of bell peppers are the exact same vegetable just at various stages of ripeness! The green bell pepper is the youngest, the yellow and orange peppers are a little further along in the ripening process, and the red peppers are the most mature.

Bread-and-Butter Pickled Salad (page 162) is a thing of beauty based on one made by my blogger buddy, Meseidy, of The Noshery years ago. I very gently altered her already excellent recipe to suit what I had on hand and loved it so much, I stuck with my changes. You're going to want to have a jar of this on hand at all times, because boy, oh, boy is this slightly sweet, definitely savory salad good and it also doubles as a sandwich or rice bowl topper.

My younger brother, Luke, has a recipe for peppers and onions that is so good, so revolutionary, and so delicious that I'm thrilled he's letting me share it. When you've had Luke's Not-So-Basic Peppers and Onions (page 165), I'm sure you'll agree!

And Herbed Goat Cheese Bell "Poppers" (page 166)—a more sophisticated and subtle cousin to the original hot pepper popper—is a two-fer recipe. You get crunchy fresh mini peppers stuffed with a garlicky herbed goat cheese and a tiny drizzle of honey to make the goat cheese sing, but you can take those same peppers and pop them through a hot oven just long enough to heat the goat cheese up and soften the peppers ever so slightly. Either way, you're going to love these!

SHOPPING TIPS: Look for firm, evenly colored peppers, with no soft spots.

STORAGE: Store the peppers in perforated plastic bags (or containers with air holes) in the crisper drawer of your refrigerator. If the peppers do not come in a perforated bag, you can create your own by snipping a few small v-shaped holes in a zip-top storage bag. You can expect yellow, red, or orange bell peppers to be good for about 4 to 5 days, and green ones to be good for a week.

BREAD-AND-BUTTER *Pickled Salad*

This tangy, refrigerated salad recipe is a little loaves-and-fishes like. You start with a couple of bell peppers, a cucumber, some onions, garlic, and a homemade brine and end up with a gorgeous, visually stunning salad reminiscent of your favorite bread-and-butter pickle that is good in the fridge for far longer than you'd ever be able to keep from eating it. It's great with everything but particularly shines on the side of grilled chicken or pork or on hot dogs or grilled sausages.

YIELD: 8 SIDE-DISH SERVINGS OR 1 QUART (960 ML) IF USING AS A CONDIMENT

INGREDIENTS

2 cups (480 ml) apple cider vinegar

1 cup (240 ml) water

1 cup (200 g) granulated sugar

2 tbsp (36 g) kosher salt

1 cup (150 g) ice cubes

1 English cucumber, cut in half lengthwise and seeded, cut into 3-4-inch (7-10-cm) segments (see Notes)

1 small red onion, ends trimmed and skin removed, cut in half and then into thin half-moons

1 lb (454 g) assorted bell peppers, stems and seeds removed, cut into thin strips (see Notes)

8 large cloves of garlic, peeled and thinly sliced

3 tbsp (33 g) whole yellow mustard seeds

½ tsp whole black peppercorns

Combine the vinegar, water, sugar, and salt in a 2-quart (2-L) saucepan over medium-high heat and stir until the sugar and salt are completely dissolved and the mixture is hot. Move the pan off of the heat and add the ice cubes to cool the mixture. Set aside.

Cut the cucumber segments into thin strips lengthwise and add those to a large mixing bowl. Add the onion and peppers along with the garlic, mustard seeds, and peppercorns and toss everything together. Stuff the vegetables into either 2 glass quart (960-ml) jars or a single glass, half-gallon (1.8-L) jar. Pour the brine over the vegetables, cover tightly, and refrigerate for at least 3 days before eating. The brine should rise to cover the vegetables after the first day, but if you find it is still too low, you can combine 2 parts apple cider vinegar to 1 part water to top off the mixture.

This pickled salad keeps for up to 4 months (yes, FOUR MONTHS!) in the refrigerator.

NOTES

To seed the English cucumber, split it in half and use a spoon to scrape out the small seed area.

Use an assortment of colors of bell peppers for optimal visual pop. You can use full-sized ones or miniature ones, just keep the weight in mind.

LUKE'S NOT-SO-BASIC
Peppers and Onions

My not-so-little brother makes some of the best fried peppers and onions around and I am thrilled to share the recipe with you. Luke is a former chef who has turned his hand to being a college lecturer, but he still has his kitchen chops. When he makes this, I am there with fork in hand waiting for them to be done. They're so good, I don't even care what else he serves with them, but boy are they amazing with grilled or broiled sausages. Most recipes have you start the peppers and onions in fat, but Luke's method develops extra-fantastic caramelized, concentrated flavors by starting the onions in a screaming hot, dry pan.

YIELD: 4 SERVINGS

INGREDIENTS

2 onions, ends trimmed and peeled, cut in half and then into ½-inch (13-mm) thick strips and separated

1 tsp kosher salt

2 tbsp (30 ml) Luke's Infused Rosemary Oil (page 246)

4 bell peppers, stems and seeds removed, sliced into ½-inch (13-mm) thick strips

1 clove of garlic, peeled and thinly sliced

½ tsp freshly ground black pepper

3 tbsp (45 ml) red wine vinegar

Place a 12-inch (30-cm) cast-iron or heavy-bottomed stainless-steel skillet over high heat. Toss in the onions, sprinkle with salt, and fry for 2 minutes, undisturbed. Then, use tongs or a long-handled wooden spoon to stir them nearly constantly for 2 minutes. You may get a little smoke happening, and that is fine.

Drizzle the oil over the onions, toss in the peppers, reduce the heat to low and continue to pan fry the onions and peppers until they are both crisp-tender and showing caramelization, about 4 minutes. Stir in the garlic and pepper and cook for 1 more minute.

Remove the pan from the heat, pour in the red wine vinegar and stir, scraping the bottom of the pan. Serve immediately.

NOTES

If you want to make these a little extra spectacular, stir in a teaspoon of bacon fat at the end before you hit the peppers and onions with the vinegar.

Leftover peppers and onions can roll quite nicely into a soup or pasta sauce.

HERBED GOAT CHEESE *Bell "Poppers"*

Mini bell peppers are the star of the show here in these savory but not-at-all spicy cousins to jalapeño poppers. This recipe is a two-fer, as it can be served cold or warm, with two wildly different and equally sublime textures and results.

YIELD 6 SERVINGS

INGREDIENTS

3 cloves of roasted garlic (see Notes)

12 oz (340 g) chevre-style goat cheese, softened to room temperature

1 tbsp (15 ml) fresh lemon juice

3 tbsp (11 g) minced fresh parsley

1 tbsp (3 g) minced fresh chives

12 mini bell peppers

1 tbsp (15 ml) mild honey

½ tsp coarse Maldon sea salt flakes (see Notes)

SERVE WITH

Grilled chicken or warm with roast chicken, pork, or beef

In a mixing bowl, use a wooden spoon to smash the roasted garlic into a paste. Add the room-temperature goat cheese and the lemon juice and vigorously stir until it is evenly combined. Stir in the parsley and chives. Set aside.

Split the bell peppers lengthwise, leaving the stems intact and scooping out any seeds. Spoon the goat cheese filling into the bell peppers. Drizzle with the honey and sprinkle the sea salt over the peppers.

To serve as a hot side dish, after you drizzle with the honey, hold off on the salt and bake in a preheated 400°F (204°C) oven on a parchment-lined pan for 10 minutes, or until hot through. Sprinkle with the salt and serve warm.

NOTES

For some variety, you can stir 2 finely chopped artichoke hearts into the cheese mixture before stuffing the peppers.

Refer to the recipe for Whipped Feta–Stuffed Cherry Tomatoes (page 65) for instructions on how to roast garlic.

Maldon sea salt flakes are large, thin, uneven, crunchy, clean-tasting salt flakes meant for finishing food. If you cannot find this, you can substitute other sea salt flakes, but do so to taste.

BALSAMIC-DRESSED FRENCH
Bell Pepper Sauté

It is impossible to have too many ways to use up bell peppers because they're abundant and economical, and they're awfully pretty to look at, too! This quick sauté is topped with a beautiful balsamic glaze that's prepared right in the same pan and is found at our table often, because it pairs beautifully with roast, grilled, or pan-fried chicken and steaks.

YIELD: 6 SERVINGS

. . . .

INGREDIENTS

3 tbsp (45 ml) Luke's Infused Garlic Oil (page 246)

1-each red, orange, and yellow bell pepper, sliced lengthwise into ½-inch (1.3-cm)-thick strips

1 clove of garlic, peeled and thinly sliced

3 tbsp (45 ml) balsamic vinegar

½ tsp freshly ground black pepper

¼ tsp kosher salt

1 tsp minced fresh parsley, for garnish

1 tsp minced fresh chives, for garnish

Place a 12-inch (30-cm) skillet over medium heat and drizzle in the oil. Swirl the pan to coat, heat until the oil is shimmery, and add in the peppers and garlic, tossing to coat. Sauté the peppers for 5 minutes, or until crisp-tender.

Transfer to a serving dish and return the pan to the burner, raising the heat to high. Stir in the vinegar, pepper, and salt, and scrape the pan, bringing the mixture to a boil. Remove the pan from the heat and drizzle the balsamic glaze over the peppers. Garnish with fresh herbs and serve.

GREEN BEANS

Green beans are at their very best in these four recipes that make the most of their natural snap, whether they're of the haricots verts or "American" variety.

Haricots verts quite literally means green beans in French. While they're the same in name, in practice, they are longer, thinner beans that have a more robust green bean flavor and tender texture. For the most part, they're interchangeable with "American" green beans. Frozen beans are undeniably convenient, but cannot be substituted for fresh beans unless noted.

Roasted Ginger-Sesame Green Beans (page 172) take long, thin haricots verts and roast them at high heat and pair them with the zesty bite of fresh ginger and toasted sesame seeds. They're fancy enough for special occasions, but easy and delicious enough to eat every night!

Cold Marinated Green Bean and Cucumber Salad (page 179) starts with frozen or blanched fresh green beans, pairs them with crunchy, refreshing cucumbers, flavorful green onions, and a quick white balsamic dressing. This is fantastic served with grilled meats and fish.

And when I tell you you're going to want a jar of Fire-and-Ice Quick-Pickled Green Beans (page 180) around all the time, I mean it. These spicy and sweet, super-crunchy green beans are extra refreshing served super chilled with either grilled meats or roasts and boy, are they easy to make!

SHOPPING TIPS: Select beans that are even in color and crisp enough to snap in half. Avoid browning, limp, and/or bruised beans.

STORAGE: Beans are best stored in a reusable container or zip-top bag in the crisper drawer of your refrigerator for up to a week.

NOTE: Green beans are ethylene sensitive.

ROASTED GINGER–SESAME
Green Beans

These tasty, crave-worthy green beans are my go-to when I don't know what else to make for dinner. They're amazing made with both fresh or frozen green beans. The real key is in the method; a pan that heats up while the oven preheats, lightly dressed beans, and BAM into the oven. A couple of shakes of the pan while the beans roast, and before long you have these crisp-tender beans that somehow go with every type of food even though they're Asian inspired.

YIELD: 6 SERVINGS

INGREDIENTS

1 lb (454 g) haricots verts

1 tbsp (15 ml) neutral oil (grapeseed, pure or light olive oil, canola, or vegetable oil)

2 tsp (10 ml) toasted sesame oil

2-3 cloves of garlic, peeled and thinly sliced or minced

1 tsp grated fresh ginger root or ginger paste

½ tsp kosher salt

1 tsp toasted sesame seeds, for serving, optional

1 green onion, roots trimmed, thinly sliced, for serving, optional

Preheat the oven to 450°F (232°C) with a rack in the middle position. Place a rimmed half-sheet pan in the oven to preheat with it.

When the oven is hot, toss together the green beans, neutral oil, sesame oil, garlic, ginger, and salt. Spread the beans over the preheated pan, making sure there is room for air to circulate around them. Roast for 16 to 20 minutes or until the beans are crisp-tender and starting to brown around the edges. Garnish with sesame seeds and green onion, if desired. Serve hot, warm, or room temperature.

SKILLET *Green Beans* WITH BACON

High on my list of most craveable foods is Skillet Green Beans with Bacon. It is so simple to make that it hardly seems possible for it to deliver such incredible flavor and texture. It's as easy as frying up a little bacon, then adding fresh green beans to the hot bacon grease and stirring until they're blistered and tender, adding in some minced shallot for a quick spin in the pan, then a wee bit of sugar or honey, and a little vinegar at the end to brighten the whole thing up. My goodness, but it is delicious with a roast of any sort, be it lamb, beef, chicken, or turkey.

YIELD: 6 SERVINGS

INGREDIENTS

6 slices thick-cut bacon

1 lb (454 g) green beans or haricots verts, ends trimmed

½ tsp kosher salt

1 large shallot, peeled and minced or ½ cup (80 g) minced purple onion

1 tsp sugar or honey

⅓ cup (80 ml) water

3 tbsp (45 ml) apple cider vinegar

½ tsp freshly ground black pepper

Lay out the bacon slices in a single layer in a cold, heavy-bottomed skillet. Place the skillet over medium heat and fry the bacon until crispy, about 15 minutes, give or take a couple of minutes. Use tongs to transfer the bacon to a paper towel–lined plate. If you have more than about 2 tablespoons (30 ml) of bacon fat, pour it off into a container. Coarsely chop the bacon and set aside.

Return the pan to the burner and adjust the heat to high. Add in the green beans and sprinkle with salt. Toss to coat. Sauté the green beans for 4 to 5 minutes, stirring frequently, until blistered. Toss in the shallot and sauté, stirring constantly, until fragrant, about 2 minutes. Add in the sugar and water, stir quickly and then tightly cover the pan and cook for 2 minutes.

Remove the lid and stir the green beans. If they are tender, use tongs to transfer them to a serving plate. Return the pan to the heat and add the vinegar and pepper. Boil until the liquid is reduced by half, about 1 minute. Crumble the bacon over the green beans, pour the sauce over the green beans, and serve.

GREEN BEANS AND CHEESE *Casserole* WITH GREEN ONION CROUTONS

If you're a fan of mac and cheese, and you're keen on green beans, you're going to love this combination! We're talking tender green beans in our Cheese Sauce of Champions (page 251) topped with fabulous green onion croutons, and baked until the sauce is bubbly and the croutons are golden brown and crunchy. It doesn't get much better than that!

SERVES 8

INGREDIENTS

2 lbs (907 g) fresh haricots verts or green beans, or frozen (See Note)

2 cups (180 g) stale bread torn into ½- to 1-inch (1.25- to 2.5-cm) pieces

3 tbsp (45 ml) Luke's Infused Garlic Oil (page 246) or extra-virgin olive oil

4 green onions, roots trimmed, thinly sliced

3 cups (720 ml) hot Cheese Sauce of Champions (page 251)

⅛ tsp freshly ground nutmeg

SERVE WITH

Roast or grilled chicken or turkey

Preheat the oven to 375°F (190°C).

If using fresh haricots verts or green beans, bring a large pot of salted water to a boil. Working in 2 batches, boil the beans for 3 to 4 minutes, or just until tender. Transfer the green beans to an ice water bath to halt the cooking. Drain well and transfer to a mixing bowl.

In a separate bowl, toss together the bread pieces and the oil, then toss in the thinly sliced green onions. Add the Cheese Sauce of Champions and nutmeg to the bowl with the green beans and toss to evenly coat. Transfer to a 2-quart baking dish and top with the green onion and bread mixture.

Bake until the cheese sauce is bubbly and the green onion croutons are golden brown. Serve hot.

NOTE

If you're using frozen green beans or haricots vert, please thaw in the refrigerator overnight before using them in this recipe.

COLD MARINATED GREEN BEAN AND CUCUMBER *Salad*

Green beans and cucumbers are—individually—some of the things I love best to eat, but combined, I am powerless against them. This salad is on the lighter side, and fills you up without making you feel like you ate a brick. It can be made with either fresh or frozen green beans, and thanks to English (a.k.a. seedless) cucumbers being available any old time, it's a salad that is do-able year round. You can skip the sesame seeds if you prefer to do so, but the subtle nuttiness they lend the salad is divine. Serve this with broiled, grilled, or fried fish or chicken.

YIELD: 8 SERVINGS

INGREDIENTS

1 lb (454 g) fresh or frozen haricots verts (see Note)

1 English (or seedless) cucumber, thinly sliced

8 scallions, trimmed of the root ends, thinly sliced

¼ cup (60 ml) white balsamic vinegar

2 tbsp (30 ml) extra-virgin olive oil

2 tbsp (18 g) toasted sesame seeds

1 tsp kosher salt

Place the green beans in a mixing bowl along with the cucumber, scallions, vinegar, oil, sesame seeds, and salt. Toss to combine evenly, then cover and refrigerate for at least 30 minutes before serving. This is best served within 24 hours of being made but will stay good for up to 4 days.

NOTE

If using fresh green beans, steam over ½ cup (120 ml) of water in a covered pan for 4 minutes, then plunge into ice water to chill and stop cooking. If using frozen green beans, thaw in the refrigerator overnight.

FIRE-AND-ICE QUICK-PICKLED
Green Beans

These slightly sweet, spicy, tangy, crisply fresh green bean pickles can be thrown together in just minutes and last up to 6 months in the refrigerator. Talk about a payoff for a very little bit of work! These are different than your average pickled green bean (which is delicious, mind you) and you'll never want to be without them to accompany grilled meats, roasted chicken, beef, or pork, or as an ingredient for memorable salads.

YIELD: 10 SERVINGS (ABOUT 2 PINTS [440 G] GREEN BEANS)

INGREDIENTS

1 tbsp (11 g) yellow mustard seeds, divided

1 tsp crushed red pepper flakes, divided

¾ lb (330 g) fresh green beans, ends snapped off, divided

6 cloves of garlic, peeled and left whole, divided

2 cups (480 ml) apple cider vinegar or white vinegar

2 tbsp (30 g) sugar

1 tbsp (18 g) kosher salt

In three clean canning jars, divide the mustard seeds, 1 teaspoon per jar, then the red pepper flakes, about a heaping ¼ teaspoon per jar, then the beans equally among the jars. If needed, snap the beans shorter so that they're no taller than ¼-inch (6-mm) below the rim of the jar. Stuff 2 cloves of garlic into each jar of beans. Set the jars aside.

In a stainless steel, or other non-reactive saucepan, bring the vinegar to a boil over medium-high heat. Remove from the burner and stir in the sugar and salt until dissolved then carefully pour over the green beans in the jars. Tightly fix lids in place and let the jars cool to room temperature before transferring to the refrigerator.

NOTES

While the beans are technically ready in 24 hours, they taste magnificent if you can wait a full week before digging into them. They will last 6 months in the refrigerator.

RADISHES

A fresh radish with a smear of soft butter and a sprinkling of coarse sea salt is one of my great joys, but radishes are so much more than just a crunchy, peppery, bite-size vegetable.

There are a surprising number of types of radishes. The most commonly found is the garden variety (see what I did there?) cherry-belle; a dark red, small, round radish. Increasingly available is the heirloom French breakfast radish with its elongated shape and pretty white tip that graduates to a red crown. You can use either of these types in all of the recipes in this book. While the large, white Daikon radishes are delicious and pretty easy to find in well-stocked grocery stores or Asian grocers, they're not suitable for the recipes here.

Crispy Roasted Radishes and Onions (page 188) harness the high heat of roasting to turn spicy radishes into a mild, sweet, crispy-edged-yet-tender revelation. They're a perfect pairing for roasts and braised meat.

Tart and tangy, blush-pink Quickled Radishes (page 191) are slightly tamer than their fresh counterparts, but retain the crunch and the peppery deliciousness. These crisp, paper-thin pickles are wonderful next to roasts and grilled meats, on tacos, salads, and sandwiches.

SHOPPING TIPS: Look for firm, un-split, moist radishes.

STORAGE: If your radishes come with the greens still attached, cut them away. Wash the radishes thoroughly and store submerged in water in a container in the refrigerator for up to 2 weeks. Change the water if it becomes cloudy as radishes are ethylene sensitive.

CREAMY RADISH DILL *Salad*

When I need a side dish to serve with grilled or fried fish, or roasted chicken, I find myself turning to this Creamy Radish Dill Salad time and again. The herby sour cream dressing tames some of the peppery bite of fresh, crunchy radishes, but it doesn't mute it completely, so you get a salad that's both beautiful and refreshing!

YIELD: 4 SERVINGS

INGREDIENTS

3 bunches of fresh radishes (about 3 lbs [1.4 kg]), greens removed, thinly sliced using a mandoline or the slicing blade of a food processor

¾ cup (180 ml) sour cream

3 tbsp (45 ml) white wine vinegar

1 tbsp (7 g) minced fresh dill

½ tsp sugar

½ tsp kosher salt

¼ tsp freshly ground black pepper

Toss the sliced radishes with the sour cream, vinegar, dill, sugar, salt, and pepper. Serve as is or over greens as a dressing.

HERBY BROWN RICE AND *Radish Salad* WITH SHAVED GRUYERE

Do yourself a favor and make this today. This salad is a delight of textures and flavors with the cold, tender rice, crunchy, peppery radishes, nutty gruyere cheese, toasty sliced almonds, and fresh herbs. This is the bees-knees with roasted or grilled lamb or chicken.

YIELD: 6 SERVINGS

INGREDIENTS

2 cups (372 g) cold, cooked brown rice (see Notes)

1 bunch radishes (about 1 lb [454 g]), thinly sliced

¼ cup (17 g) sliced almonds, toasted (see Notes)

¼ cup (13 g) fresh dill, finely chopped

4 green onions, roots trimmed, thinly sliced

¼ cup + 1 tbsp (75 ml) Mason Jar Vinaigrette (page 248)

2 oz (57 g) aged gruyere cheese, shaved with a vegetable peeler

In a mixing bowl, use your hands to separate the grains of cold rice. Toss in the radishes, almonds, dill, and green onions. Drizzle the vinaigrette over the mixture, add in the cheese, and toss to coat. Serve immediately.

NOTES

I like this best prepared with short grain brown rice, but it is also good prepared with long-grain brown rice. Experiment a bit to find your preference. The real key is that the rice must be chilled thoroughly for this salad.

To toast the almonds, place the sliced almonds in a dry pan over medium heat. Toast for 3 to 5 minutes, stirring with a wooden spoon and shaking the pan frequently, just until they are fragrant. Be careful, though, as they are prone to burning quickly! Transfer the nuts to a plate immediately.

CRISPY *Roasted Radishes* AND ONIONS

Radishes can be polarizing, but I'm on the mission to make everyone love them, and these Roasted Radishes and Onions are just the way to do it. Tender, crisp-on-the-outside, sweet, and mild—Yes! Mild!—and sublime enough to convert even the biggest radish hater! Serve these with roast or grilled lamb, beef, or pork.

YIELD: 6 SERVINGS

INGREDIENTS

2 large bunches radishes (about 1 lb [454 g] each) trimmed of the greens, halved or quartered if larger than 1 inch (2.5 cm)

1 lb (454 g) spring onions or small onions, cut into wedges the same size as the radish pieces

1 tbsp (15 ml) Luke's Infused Chive Oil (page 246) or extra-virgin olive oil

½ tsp kosher salt

½ tsp coarsely ground black pepper

Preheat the oven to 425°F (220°C). Pile the radishes and onions onto a rimmed cookie sheet or cast-iron skillet.

Drizzle the oil over the vegetables, sprinkle the salt and black pepper over the top and toss to coat, spreading the radishes and onions out into a single layer. Roast for 10 minutes then lower the heat to 350°F (176°C), and stir the vegetables. Roast for 20 to 30 more minutes, stirring every 10 minutes, or until the vegetables are deeply caramelized on the outside and tender on the inside. These can be served hot or room temperature.

QUICKLED *Radishes*

Quickly pickled radishes—or Quickled Radishes—are an easy peasy, tart and tangy way to use up the radishes that are absolutely everywhere during the summer. The pretty-in-pink radish pickles are still full of flavor, but have some of their peppery bite tamed by the pickling process. Even though they're ready to eat as soon as they cool, the longer they sit, the tastier they get. I love these on salads, tacos, sandwiches, and just piled on a plate alongside any and all grilled meats.

YIELD: 8 SERVINGS (1-PINT [480-ML] JAR)

INGREDIENTS

1 lb (454 g) radishes, trimmed of greens and scrubbed, thinly sliced using a mandoline or sharp knife

5 cloves of garlic, peeled and lightly smacked with a knife to crack them open

½ tsp whole black peppercorns, lightly cracked with a pan (see Note)

1 cup (240 ml) water

1 cup (240 ml) apple cider vinegar

2 tsp (8 g) sugar or (10 ml) honey

2 tsp (6 g) kosher salt

Pack the radishes into a jar with a tight-fitting lid along with the garlic cloves and black peppercorns.

Add the water, vinegar, sugar, and salt to a stainless steel or other non-reactive saucepan over high heat. Bring to a boil, and cook just until the sugar and salt are dissolved. Pour over the radishes and garlic. Cover and let cool to room temperature then refrigerate. These Quickled Radishes store well in the refrigerator for up to a month.

NOTE

To keep your peppercorns from skittering across the counter when you smack them with a pan to crack them, wrap them in a clean kitchen towel before hitting them. You're not looking to pulverize them, just bruise them up a bit to release the oils.

CABBAGE

Unlike sprouts, larger is milder and sweeter when it comes to most cabbages. And if you have an in with the local farmer or market, you should be aware that green cabbage harvested after the first frost will be sweeter.

Green and purple cabbage are probably what you first think of when you think about cabbage; crunchy, peppery, their sturdiness makes them ideal for slaws, roasting, and pan-frying. Cooking the cabbage brings out the sweetness in it.

Napa cabbage (a.k.a. Chinese cabbage) is elongated and has thick stems with frilly leaves. It is sweet and is wonderful raw, marinated (like in our Quick Kimchi, page 198), and in stir-fries.

Savoy cabbage is the beauty queen of the cabbage world with its frilly, frizzly dark green exterior that graduates to a lighter yellow, then cream-colored center. This is another cabbage that is good both raw and cooked, and is the most tender of the bunch.

Thai Peanut Slaw (page 194) gives a starring role to red cabbage, and when I am looking for what to do with a head of green cabbage, I almost always reach for Grandma Val's Cranberry-Almond Coleslaw (page 197).

SHOPPING TIPS: Fresh cabbage is shiny and bright/deep in color. Green cabbage should be so green it is almost lime, while red cabbage will be a deep, dark purple. Savoy cabbage will be a bright green. Napa cabbage will have shiny white stems, and healthy, non-wilted pale green or yellowish-green leaves. All cabbage should feel heavy for its size and have firm, compact, and crisp leaves. Avoid cabbage with browning or yellowed (not be to be confused with the healthy yellowish green of Napa cabbage) leaves.

STORAGE: Green, red, and Savoy cabbage should all be stored in plastic bags in the refrigerator. Napa cabbage is best when wrapped in a single layer of plastic wrap surrounding the whole cabbage and stashed in the refrigerator. Most varieties of cabbage will give you at least 1 week of freshness when stored properly, with green cabbage taking the lead and remaining in satisfactory condition for up to 2 weeks.

Note: Cabbages are ethylene sensitive.

THAI PEANUT *Slaw*

Red cabbage is the colorful star in this wildly flavorful slaw that has
loads of texture and crunch courtesy of vegetables and chopped peanuts.
Serve this rainbow veggie slaw with grilled chicken, fish, or pork.

YIELD: 8 SERVINGS

INGREDIENTS

3 cups (210 g) shredded red
cabbage

2 cups (170 g) julienned or roughly
shredded raw broccoli stems or
green cabbage

1 cup (110 g) matchstick carrots

1 red, yellow, or orange bell pepper,
stem and seeds removed, sliced
into thin strips

½ cup (8 g) fresh cilantro leaves

3 green onions, thinly sliced

1 red Fresno chili pepper, stem
and seeds removed, finely minced,
optional

⅓ cup (49 g) salted peanuts,
chopped

¼ cup (60 ml) rice wine vinegar

2 tbsp (30 ml) fresh lime juice

2 tbsp (30 ml) honey

1 tbsp (15 ml) toasted sesame oil

1 tbsp (15 ml) fish sauce

1½ tsp (7 g) grated fresh ginger

1 small clove of garlic, peeled and
minced

In a large mixing bowl, toss together the cabbage, broccoli, carrots, bell
pepper, cilantro, green onions, Fresno chili pepper, if using, and chopped
peanuts. Set aside.

In a jar with a tight-fitting lid, shake together the vinegar, lime juice, honey,
sesame oil, fish sauce, ginger, and garlic. Toss half of the dressing with the
slaw and refrigerate for at least 10 minutes before serving. Stir or shake well
and serve with additional dressing at the table.

Store leftovers in the refrigerator, tightly covered, for up to 4 days.

GRANDMA VAL'S CRANBERRY–ALMOND *Coleslaw*

My stepmom Val, or Grandma Val as the kids called her, was a wizard in the kitchen and everyone loved this sweet and savory, textural delight of a coleslaw with tart but sweet dried cranberries and toasted, sliced almonds.

YIELD: 8 SERVINGS

INGREDIENTS

½ cup (120 ml) mayonnaise

1 tbsp (15 g) granulated sugar

1 tbsp (15 ml) white vinegar or lemon juice

½ tsp kosher salt

½ tsp freshly ground black pepper

5 cups (350 g) shredded green cabbage

1 carrot, shredded

¼ cup (30 g) dried cranberries

2 tbsp (14 g) toasted slivered almonds

½ tsp celery seed, optional, but tasty

SERVE WITH

Grilled sausages, ham, or roast chicken

In a small mixing bowl, whisk together the mayonnaise, sugar, vinegar, salt, and pepper until smooth. Set aside.

In a large mixing bowl, toss together the cabbage, carrot, cranberries, almonds, and celery seed, if using. Pour the dressing over the cabbage and toss to coat. This can be served immediately, or can be stored, tightly covered, in the refrigerator for up to 4 days. Be sure to toss/stir the slaw well before serving after refrigerating.

NOTE

If you'd like to lighten this coleslaw up a bit, you can sub in plain Greek yogurt for half of the mayonnaise. It's really excellent and just slightly different.

QUICK *Kimchi*

While true kimchi needs a couple of days to ferment at room temperature before it's ready, this quick kimchi will help you scratch the kimchi itch in just an hour. And if you're a little leery of the majestic funk kimchi brings with it, you should give this fast version a try; it is definitely far less funkadelic while still packing all of the spicy, flavorful power of the fermented version. Serve this with Asian main dishes, roasted or fried chicken, steaks, or with grilled fish.

YIELD: 8 SERVINGS

INGREDIENTS

1 lb (454 g) Napa cabbage, core removed, chopped into 1–2-inch (3–5-cm) pieces

1 lb (454 g) savoy cabbage, core removed, chopped into 1–2-inch (3–5-cm) pieces

6 green onions, roots trimmed, split in half lengthwise, cut into 1–2-inch (3–5-cm) pieces

1 carrot, shredded

⅓ cup (90 g) kosher salt

¼ cup + 1 tsp (55 g) granulated sugar, divided

2 cloves of garlic, peeled and minced

1 tsp (5 g) grated fresh ginger

1 tbsp (6 g) Korean chili flakes (gochugaru) or crushed red pepper flakes

2 tbsp (30 ml) fish sauce

1 tbsp (15 ml) toasted sesame oil

Toasted sesame seeds, for garnish, optional

Mix the Napa and savoy cabbage, green onions, and carrot in a large, stainless steel or glass mixing bowl. Set aside.

In a large saucepan, combine 2 quarts (2 L) of water, salt, and ¼ cup (50 g) of the sugar together over medium heat, stirring until the salt and sugar are completely dissolved and it is warm to the touch. Pour the brine over the vegetables and toss to coat. Cover loosely and let stand at room temperature for 30 minutes.

Drain the vegetables in a colander and rinse with cold running water. Rinse the bowl you used to brine the vegetables and return the vegetables to it. Add the garlic, ginger, red pepper flakes, fish sauce, sesame oil, and final teaspoon of sugar and stir to combine evenly. Again, cover loosely and let stand at room temperature for 30 minutes.

Kimchi can be served immediately, garnished with toasted sesame seeds before serving if desired, or kept, covered, in the refrigerator for up to 2 weeks.

NOTE

If either Napa or savoy cabbage is unavailable, sub in an equal amount of the one you can find at the store. The mix of textures is nice, but not strictly necessary.

CABBAGE, BACON, AND APPLE
Roast Up

Easy, easy, easy and oh so tasty, our roast up is full of sweet, roasted cabbage, smoky bacon, and pieces of sweet, tender apples. It's an homage to a great version that my friend Mary of Barefeet in the Kitchen makes that contains Brussels sprouts but uses a good old-fashioned green cabbage instead. We love this comforting autumnal side dish with roasted or grilled sausages or pork chops, but it's also fantastic alongside roast chicken.

YIELD: 4 TO 6 SERVINGS

INGREDIENTS

5 slices thick-cut bacon, cut into 1-inch (3-cm) pieces

1 small head of cabbage (about 1½ lbs [680 g]), cut into bite-size pieces (see Note)

½ tsp kosher salt

½ tsp coarsely ground black pepper

1 firm, juicy apple (I love Empires, Fujis, and Galas for this recipe)

2 tsp (10 ml) apple cider vinegar

Preheat the oven to 425°F (220°C). Scatter the bacon in a single layer on a rimmed half-sheet pan. Bake for 10 minutes, or until the bacon is cooked through, but not crisp at all.

Use a slotted spoon to remove the bacon from the sheet pan and set aside on a plate. Try to keep all of the bacon drippings on the pan. Add the cabbage pieces to the pan and toss well, trying to coat them evenly in the bacon fat. Sprinkle the cabbage with salt and pepper. Roast for 15 minutes, or until the cabbage begins to brown at the edges.

Add the apple pieces and the cooked bacon to the cabbage on the pan and toss to coat. Roast until the cabbage and apples are tender and the bacon is crisped, about 10 to 15 minutes. As soon as you pull the pan from the oven, sprinkle with the vinegar and toss to coat. Serve immediately!

NOTE

For a detailed description of how to best cut the cabbage into bite-size pieces check out Let Me Break It Down For You! (page 258).

Pickled Carrots Two Ways:
GINGER–PICKLED CARROTS

You're going to find yourself putting these Asian-inspired pickled carrot sticks with all sorts of meals; stir-fries and rice bowls are natural pairings for the tangy, lightly gingery, crisp-tender carrot strips. And bonus! As long as the carrots are covered by brine, they're good for up to a year in the refrigerator.

YIELD: 8 SERVINGS (ABOUT 2 JARS, 1 PINT [480 ML] EACH)

INGREDIENTS

1 cup (240 ml) unseasoned rice vinegar (see Notes)

¾ cup (180 ml) water

6 long, thin strips (about 3–4-inch [7–10-cm] each) of peeled, fresh ginger root

2 whole star anise

⅓ cup (67 g) raw or granulated sugar

1½ tsp (2 g) crushed red pepper flakes

1 clove of garlic, peeled and minced

½ tsp kosher salt

1 lb (454 g) of peeled carrots, cut into matchsticks ¼ x 3-inch (6-mm x 7-cm) pieces using a mandoline (see Notes)

In a stainless steel—or other non-reactive pot—combine the vinegar, water, ginger, star anise, sugar, red pepper flakes, garlic, and salt. Bring to a boil, stirring just until the sugar is dissolved. Use a slotted spoon to remove the star anise from the boiling brine and divide them evenly between two clean pint jars.

Add the carrot sticks to the brine. Bring the liquid back to a boil, about 2 minutes. Turn off the heat. Immediately use tongs or a slotted spoon to divide the carrot sticks between the jars, also putting 3 strips of ginger in each jar, packing if necessary, to fit them all in. Use a ladle to pour the hot brine over the carrot sticks, being sure to cover them with brine. Insert a sterile chopstick or knife into the jars to release air bubbles and add more brine, if necessary, to cover the carrots. Put a new, two-piece lid on each jar and let them come to room temperature before transferring to the refrigerator.

NOTES

Be sure to use unseasoned rice vinegar for these pickles and not seasoned rice vinegar which contains sugar and salt.

If you don't have a mandoline, you can cut long thin strips of the carrots with a vegetable peeler and cut those down into thinner strips This will not be quite the same visually, but it is a nice solution if you lack the equipment.

Pickled Carrots Two Ways:
MEDITERRANEAN–PICKLED CARROTS

Delightfully flavored with garlic, lemon, and oregano, these super-fresh pickled carrots will pair beautifully with grilled or roasted chicken or fish. I love them on salads and tucked into sandwiches, too. And just like the Ginger-Pickled Carrots, these are good for up to a year in the refrigerator as long as the carrots stay submerged in the brine.

YIELD: 8 SERVINGS (ABOUT 2 JARS, 1 PINT [480 ML] EACH)

INGREDIENTS

1 whole lemon, scrubbed and cut into eight wedges (see Notes)

4 sprigs fresh oregano, washed

1 cup (240 ml) white wine vinegar

¾ cup (180 ml) water

⅓ cup (66 g) raw or granulated sugar

1½ tsp (2 g) crushed red pepper flakes

4 cloves of garlic, peeled and smacked lightly to break up slightly

1 tsp kosher salt

1 lb (454 g) of peeled carrots, cut into matchsticks ¼ x 3–inch (6-mm x 7-cm) pieces using a mandoline (see Notes)

Divide the lemon wedges and sprigs of oregano between two clean pint jars. Set aside.

In a stainless steel—or other non-reactive pot—combine the vinegar, water, sugar, red pepper flakes, garlic, and salt. Bring to a boil, stirring just until the sugar is dissolved. Use a slotted spoon to remove the garlic from the brine and divide them evenly between the jars.

Add the carrot sticks to the boiling brine. Bring the liquid back to a boil, about 2 minutes. Turn off the heat. Immediately use tongs or a slotted spoon to divide the carrot sticks between the jars, packing, if necessary, to fit them all in. Use a ladle to pour the hot brine over the carrot sticks, being sure to cover completely. Insert a sterile chopstick or knife into the jars to release air bubbles and add more brine, if necessary, to cover the carrots. Put a new, two-piece lid on each jar and let them come to room temperature before transferring to the refrigerator.

NOTES

It's best to use organic lemons for this since you're adding it—peel and all—to the jars.

If you don't have a mandoline, you can cut long thin strips of the carrots with a vegetable peeler and cut those down into thinner strips. This will not be quite the same visually, but it is a nice solution if you lack the equipment.

ONIONS and HERBS

Onions and herbs are where the flavor is in every meal, as far as I am concerned. A little bit of them in almost every dish makes the difference between fab and drab.

I've cut all of the chaff out of every casserole ever built and kept only what I love the best: the onions and the cheese. Herculean amounts of melted cheese, a little garlic, and some fresh herbs are all that is needed to shed the spotlight on savory onions in The "Best Part of Any Casserole" Onion Casserole (page 216).

On the lighter side, we have Quick-Pickled Red Onions (page 219), which bring freshness and crunch to any dish they accompany; Grilled Pineapple and Sweet Onions (page 220), which deliver huge, Hawaiian-inspired flavor with very little work; and Grilled Green Onions (page 224), which just might be the easiest side dish ever to impress.

For something that splits the difference between totally indulgent and featherweight, we have satisfying Sesame Soba Noodles with Green Onions (page 223) which can be served with grilled or roasted fish or chicken.

And finally, please let me introduce you to your new, all-purpose side-dish: Red Wine Oven-Caramelized Onions (page 227) which are the easiest and best caramelized onions you'll ever taste. Whether piled high next to a grilled steak or pork roast or on top of a hamburger, you're going to find a multitude of ways to serve these sweet and savory, meltingly tender onions.

SHOPPING TIPS: Bulbs should be firm, heavy for their size, and have little to no scent. Avoid onions and garlic with cuts, blemishes, bruises, soft spots, or strong odor.

STORAGE: Onion and garlic bulbs stored in a cool, dry, dark, well-ventilated place will be good for 1 to 2 months in the summer and up to 6 months in the winter. The refrigerator is not ideal unless you have peeled or cut the onion. A peeled or cut onion will be good, tightly wrapped, in the refrigerator for up to a week.

FRESH HERBS AND GREEN ONIONS

I know fresh herbs aren't vegetables, but I do use quite a few of them and recommend them over dried herbs in most recipes. With just a little care, you can stretch a fresh bundle of herbs from the market or store to last much longer, so I'm including this advice.

SHOPPING TIPS: Try to stick with herbs with a deep or vibrant green color and leaves that are fresh-looking with no wilting, soft spots, or discoloration in sight. The stems should be tender and you should be able to break them with your fingers in the case of soft herbs like parsley, cilantro, basil, tarragon, dill, and mint, or woody in the case of hard herbs like rosemary, sage, thyme, chives, marjoram, and oregano, depending on the variety, and the leaves should be fragrant when pinched between your fingers.

STORAGE: With soft herbs you should trim about ¼ inch (6 mm) off of the ends of the stems, then arrange them in a jar with the stems in a couple of inches of water, much like arranging flowers. Loosely cover the leaves with a plastic bag or plastic wrap and store in the refrigerator. As long as you change the water every couple of days, you'll likely be able to get as much as 2 weeks of freshness from them.

Basil requires a little extra care. it should be kept in water and loosely wrapped as described above, but kept at room temperature where there is a little light available. It is not likely to keep as long as other soft herbs, but it doesn't do well when refrigerated.

Hard herbs last quite well when wrapped once around with paper towels and stored uncrowded in a plastic bag in the crisper drawer of your refrigerator.

Green onions are a delicious and fun anomaly. You can actually grow more green onions using the green onions you have. Simply trim the white, root end away from the green end. Use the green end in your recipes, and arrange the roots in enough water to cover the hairy roots by an inch or so. Keep them on the counter, changing the water every other day, and in about a week, you'll have more green onion tops to cut off and use. You can go on like this indefinitely. *Vive les* green onions!

THE "BEST PART OF ANY CASSEROLE"
Onion Casserole

I am the first person to admit that when you say, "Casserole." I say, "Boring!" This heavenly, habit-forming, bubbly, baked cheese-and-onion concoction, though, is the farthest thing from boring even if it is technically a casserole. It is also ridiculously easy to make and people, that's a good thing, because you're going to be serving this every chance you get. Happily, it's also made from ingredients that you can get at almost any grocery store from local convenience stores to big-city gourmet purveyors; onions, Cheddar, mozzarella, and butter. It benefits from a shower of fresh herbs at the end, but it isn't strictly necessary. Go on. Make this. I'll wait right here for you. You're going to love it! Serve this with burgers, roast ham, pork, beef, chicken, or with grilled portabella mushrooms.

YIELD: 8 SERVINGS

. . . .

INGREDIENTS

3 large onions, ends trimmed, sliced in half from north to south pole and peeled

2 cloves of garlic, peeled and thinly sliced

1 tsp kosher salt

½–¾ tsp freshly ground black pepper

4 tbsp (56 g) butter, cut into small cubes

1 cup (113 g) shredded Cheddar cheese

1 cup (112 g) shredded mozzarella cheese

1 tsp chopped fresh thyme, oregano, and/or parsley, optional but delicious

Preheat the oven to 350°F (176°C). Grease a 9 x 13–inch (23 x 33–cm) rectangular or 9-inch (23-cm) oval casserole with non-stick cooking spray or oil and set aside.

Slice the onions into ½-inch (1-cm) thick half-moons and separate the rings, tossing them into the prepared pan. Sprinkle the garlic, salt, and pepper over the onions. Scatter the butter over the onions. Mix the cheeses together and evenly distribute over the onion mixture. Bake for 30 to 40 minutes, or until the cheese is melted, bubbly, brown around the edges, and has golden-brown patches on the surface. Garnish with fresh herbs and let stand for at least 5 minutes before serving. This can be served hot or warm.

NOTE

Leftover casserole is incredible when reheated in a hot frying pan; the results are crisp edges with the beautifully melted cheese and fragrant onions. It's worth planning leftovers!

QUICK-PICKLED *Red Onions*

If I had a dime for every dish I'd ever stuffed these tangy, umami-packed, deliciously addictive little quick-pickled red onions into or next to, I'd be wealthy beyond my wildest imagination. Thankfully, they're as easy on the wallet as they are to make, and they're an instant flavor infusion for anything that needs a little oomph. Serve these alongside any and all roast meats, grilled hot dogs, sausages, fish, and chicken. They're also incredible on tacos, sandwiches, and salads of all types.

YIELD: 12 SERVINGS (APPROX. 2 PINTS [960 ML])

INGREDIENTS

10 whole peppercorns

4 whole cloves

2 tsp (8 g) whole yellow mustard seeds

2 tsp (4 g) celery seed

2 lbs (907 g) red onions, peeled and very thinly sliced

2 whole bay leaves

2 cups (480 ml) red wine vinegar

½ cup (120 ml) water

⅓ cup (66 g) sugar

1½ tsp (9 g) kosher salt

Divide the spices between two clean pint jars thusly; each jar should have 5 peppercorns, 2 cloves, 1 teaspoon of mustard seeds, and 1 teaspoon of celery seed. Divide the sliced onions between the two jars, packing gently to fit them all into the jars. Slide a bay leaf in between the onions and the wall of each jar. Set them aside.

Combine the vinegar, water, sugar, and salt in a stainless-steel saucepan over medium-high heat, stirring to dissolve the sugar. Bring the mixture to a boil, then reduce the heat to medium-low and simmer for 2 minutes.

Use a ladle to pour the boiling brine over the onions in the jar, taking your time and letting the liquid percolate through the onions. When the onions are submerged in the liquid (see Notes), wipe the rim of the jar and fix a two-piece lid in place. Let the onions cool to room temperature, then refrigerate until well-chilled. These onions will keep well in the refrigerator for up to 2 months.

NOTES:

If you run a little short of the amount of brine needed to completely cover the onions in the jars, you can add a splash of water to the jar to fill it up.

Save the leftover onion brine to add as a vinegar component to salad dressings or use in cooking.

GRILLED PINEAPPLE AND
Sweet Onions

When you absolutely, positively must deliver the most flavor with the least amount of work, this is the recipe you want to make. The high, fast heat of the grill gives a little smokiness while concentrating the sweetness of both the juicy pineapple and the fragrant onion. If you don't have a grill, don't fret; you can prepare this just as easily on a grill pan! I adore these with any kind of ham or pork, but it's also majorly impressive with grilled chicken, fish, or hamburgers.

YIELD: 8 SERVINGS

INGREDIENTS

¼ cup (60 ml) olive oil

1 tbsp (15 ml) fresh lime juice or lemon juice, plus 1 half of a lime or lemon

1 tsp honey

½ tsp kosher salt

½ tsp fresh black pepper

1 fresh pineapple, peeled and cut into 1-inch (3-cm) slabs (see Notes)

2 sweet onions, peeled and cut into 1-inch (3-cm) slabs

Preheat an outdoor grill for high, direct heat. Lightly oil the grate. Alternately, put a grill pan over medium-high heat and lightly brush it with oil.

In a small bowl, whisk together the olive oil, lime juice, honey, salt, and pepper. Brush the sauce on one side of each slab of pineapple and onion, and place on the grill or grill pan brushed side down. Brush the top of the pineapple and onion slices. Grill, undisturbed, for 2 to 4 minutes, or until you see grill marks on the pineapple and onion when you slide a spatula underneath and lift it. Gently turn the slices and grill for another 2 to 4 minutes, or until you see grill marks on the other side and they're hot through and through.

Arrange the pineapple and onion slices on a serving plate and squeeze the citrus over the top before serving.

NOTES

This recipe does not require you to core your fresh pineapple because it makes it easier to flip on the grill when the core is left intact. You'll just cut around the core when you eat it.

If you'd like to make this with canned pineapple, you can definitely do that! Simply drain the pineapple rings and proceed as directed above, but be aware the canned rings will be done faster than the fresh pineapple.

SESAME *Soba Noodles* WITH GREEN ONIONS

Versatility is the name of the game with these Sesame Soba Noodles with Green Onions. They sing as a side dish for grilled or stir-fried chicken when they're warm, or when served cold as a side dish for grilled or broiled fish. Any way you make them, you'll love the al dente bite of the buckwheat soba noodles with toasted sesame seeds and green onions. Bonus: This easy-on-the-wallet side dish doubles nicely as a vegetarian main dish or base for noodle bowls.

YIELD: 6 SERVINGS AS A SIDE DISH, 4 SERVINGS AS A MAIN DISH

. . . .

INGREDIENTS

⅓ cup (80 ml) low-sodium soy sauce

3 tbsp (45 ml) toasted sesame oil

2 tbsp (30 ml) rice vinegar

1 tbsp (15 ml) mild honey or brown sugar

1 tsp grated ginger or ginger paste

½ tsp cracked black pepper or crushed red pepper flakes for more spice

1 tbsp (15 ml) sunflower, canola, or vegetable oil

20 green onions, roots trimmed, 16 cut into ½–¾-inch (13–19-mm) pieces, the rest sliced thinly, divided

10 oz (283 g) buckwheat soba noodles, prepared according to package, drained and rinsed with cold water

2 tbsp (18 g) toasted sesame seeds, divided

In a jar, combine the soy sauce, sesame oil, vinegar, honey, ginger, and pepper. Fix a lid in place on the jar and shake to combine thoroughly. Set aside.

Heat the oil to a shimmery state in a 12-inch (30-cm) skillet over medium-high heat. Toss in the larger pieces of green onion and stir fry for 15 to 30 seconds, or until they're fragrant. Shake your soy sauce mixture and pour it into the pan, cooking for about 30 seconds, or until bubbly, then toss in the soba noodles to coat evenly and distribute the onions. Remove from the heat and toss in the rest of the green onions and 1½ tablespoons (13 g) of the sesame seeds, reserving the others for garnish.

Sprinkle the remaining sesame seeds over the top just before serving. Serve hot, room temperature, or cold. Store leftovers tightly covered in the refrigerator for up to 3 days.

NOTE

For a great twist and heartier dish, add some cooked edamame to the noodles.

GRILLED *Green Onions*

When you absolutely, positively must deliver the most flavor with the least amount of work and in the fastest time, this is the recipe you want to make. A little oil, a handful of green onions, and some heat from a grill or a grill pan converts these humble little everyday onions into a memorable side dish worthy of the most wonderful burgers, grilled sausage, chicken, or lamb.

YIELD: 4 TO 6 SERVINGS

INGREDIENTS
1 tbsp (15 ml) sunflower or olive oil
16 green onions, roots trimmed
¾ tsp kosher salt
½ tsp cracked black pepper

Preheat a grill or grill pan over medium-high heat.

Brush the oil lightly over all sides of each green onion. Sprinkle evenly with the salt and pepper.

Place the onions on the grill and cook until the greens wilt just slightly and the onions have some grill marks, about 1 to 2 minutes per side.

Transfer to a serving dish and serve immediately.

RED WINE OVEN–CARAMELIZED *Onions*

Meet your new favorite all-purpose side dish, folks, and let's demystify that alchemy that is caramelized onions. This easy method to create a tantalizing, restaurant-worthy side dish of tender, flavorful onions with endless uses. When I say you can serve this with about any main dish, I mean it. Beef, pork, chicken, lamb, mushrooms, stew, soup, or toast are all a happy pairing with these delicious morsels. It may seem like a crazy amount of onion, but it shrinks down to about ⅛th of its original volume in the oven.

YIELD: 4 SERVINGS

. . . .

INGREDIENTS

4 large red, yellow, or white onions, peeled and thinly sliced (see Notes)

4 cloves of garlic, peeled and lightly crushed but still intact

¼ cup (60 ml) dry red wine or balsamic vinegar (see Notes)

4 tbsp (60 ml) olive oil

1 tbsp (14 g) brown sugar

1½ tsp (9 g) kosher salt

1 tsp coarsely ground black pepper

4 sprigs fresh thyme or 1 tsp dried whole thyme leaves

Preheat the oven to 375°F (190°C).

In a large mixing bowl, toss together the onions, garlic, red wine, olive oil, sugar, salt, pepper, and thyme sprigs to evenly distribute. Transfer this onto a rimmed half-sheet pan. Cover the pan tightly with foil. Bake for 20 minutes, remove the pan from the oven and the foil from the pan, stir the onions, being sure to move the ones that were in the corner toward the center and vice versa. Replace the foil, return the pan to the oven, and roast for another 20 minutes before stirring again.

You'll repeat the roasting and stirring at least one more time, but up to 2 more times, depending on how well caramelized you like your onions. Remove the thyme sprigs and use the onions hot, cold, or anywhere in between. Leftovers can be refrigerated for up to 3 days, or frozen in ice cube trays and transferred to zip-top bags in the freezer for up to 3 months.

NOTES

The temptation might be strong to use sweet onions, but it is better to chance the crying and use a stronger onion for this. All of what makes you weep while cutting onions converts to deliciously sweet results when caramelized. Sweet onions just don't make the cut here and are much more delicious raw!

The choice to use a nice, drinkable, dry red wine or balsamic vinegar here is yours. They're both divine.

Since you have your oven going already, you can certainly double this recipe in 2 pans to have more onions to have on hand. They do freeze beautifully!

SWEET POTATOES

My grandma used to call my siblings, cousins, and me her "little sweet potatoes." Since my grandma was a wonderful woman who everyone adored, it was a term of endearment that encouraged me to love the humble orange tubers, too.

And in what I can only think of as a divine homage to my grandma, two of the top five most popular posts on my blog are sweet potato recipes and I'm sharing them with you here.

There aren't enough superlatives in our language to describe just how comforting Melting Sweet Potatoes (page 230) are; meltingly tender, deeply caramelized, flavor-packed sweet potatoes. The uncomplicated, high-temperature cooking method condenses both the sweet and savory qualities of sweet potatoes. Some people are a little skeptical of the addition of broth and chopped garlic until they try it, but I promise you these are incredible.

Most people have tried sweet potato fries by now, but many of us who love them have long struggled to create a baked sweet potato fry with actual crunchy exteriors and fluffy interiors. Using a method taken from making crispy baked "regular" potato fries ended up being the key. A soak of the raw fries in water to help leech out some of the starch, then toss through cornstarch or rice starch to help create a crust before going into a hot, hot oven does the job! I lead you through the process step-by-step because I love you, my little sweet potatoes!

SHOPPING TIPS: Try to select sweet potatoes with firm, unwrinkled, unblemished skin and no soft or dark spots. When considering what size to select, keep in mind that small to medium sweet potatoes are less starchy, making larger ones ideal for sweet potato fries (page 233). Small or medium sweet potatoes are better for melting sweet potatoes (page 230).

STORAGE: Sweet potatoes are a little more delicate or less hardy than white potatoes when it comes to storage. Stored at room temperature (68 to 70°F [21 to 21°C]), they're good for about a week. For longer storage, you'll need a well-ventilated, much cooler (about 55°F [13°C]), dark room like a basement or root cellar. Do not, however, refrigerate raw sweet potatoes. It will make them taste funny and make the centers of the potatoes hard and unpleasant.

MELTING *Sweet Potatoes*

Of all the wonderful ways sweet potatoes can be served, this think-outside-the-box way is my absolute favorite. Meltingly tender, deeply caramelized, and slightly savory, these sweet potatoes are a natural at any meal, festive or every day. I always try to make extra because the leftovers are wonderful on dinner salads! It's hard, though, because my appetite always seems to match or exceed the number of potatoes I've prepared. There's a reason this is one of the most popular recipes ever published on my blog. Be ready to be wowed! Serve with roasted or grilled pork, chicken, turkey, beef, or venison, spinach or mixed green salads, and strong cheese.

YIELD: 8 SERVINGS

INGREDIENTS

3 lbs (1.4 kg) sweet potatoes, peeled and cut into 1-inch (3-cm) thick rounds

3 tbsp (45 ml) melted butter or extra-virgin coconut oil

3 tbsp (45 ml) garlic or plain extra-virgin olive oil

1¼ tsp (7 g) kosher salt

1 tsp ground black pepper

3 cloves of garlic, peeled and thinly sliced

1¼ cups (300 ml) vegetable broth

Preheat the oven to 500°F (260°C).

Arrange sweet potatoes on a half-sheet pan with space between the slices to allow for air to circulate. Drizzle the potatoes with the butter and the garlic oil. Sprinkle the salt and pepper over the top. Use your hands to flip the sweet potatoes and slide them around in the oils, making sure they're completely coated.

Roast the sweet potatoes for 15 minutes, or until the undersides of the slices have caramelized to a beautiful deep brown. Carefully flip the sweet potato slices and return the pan to the oven for another 15 minutes.

Flip the sweet potato slices once again and scatter the garlic over the sweet potato slices. Pour the vegetable broth over the works. Return the pan to the oven for another 15 minutes, or until completely tender and the broth has reduced to a thicker consistency. Use a spatula to transfer the Melting Sweet Potatoes to a serving plate and drizzle the sauce from the pan over them.

NOTES

You can make these with Yukon gold potatoes in place of the sweet potatoes, too!

DO NOT USE GLASS PANS to make these. They may crack at those temperatures.

GUARANTEED CRISPY BAKED *Sweet Potato Fries*

You want crispy sweet potato fries without busting out a vat of oil? I'm your gal. These fries are the bees-knees and you'll be so glad to have sweet potato fries better than you can get at most restaurants. Serve this with burgers, steaks, hot dogs, sausages, and grilled chicken!

YIELD: 4 SERVINGS

INGREDIENTS

2 large sweet potatoes, about 12 oz (340 g) each , peeled, cut lengthwise into ¼ x ¼-inch (6 x 6-mm) matchsticks (see Notes)

4 tsp (10 g) cornstarch, divided (see Notes)

2 tbsp (30 ml) sunflower, peanut, grapeseed, or canola oil, divided

¼ tsp chipotle powder, divided, optional

Salt, to taste

Put the sweet potatoes in a bowl and cover with cold, fresh water. Let them soak for 1 hour or up to overnight in the refrigerator. Drain the sweet potato matchsticks into a colander, rinse with fresh water, then pat them dry with paper towels. They should not be visibly wet, but do not need to be bone dry.

Preheat the oven to 420°F (215°C). Line 2 half-sheet pans with heavy-duty foil, dull side up, and spritz lightly with non-stick cooking spray. Set aside.

Add half of the sweet potato sticks to a very large plastic bag. Sprinkle 2 teaspoons (5 g) of the cornstarch over the potatoes, trap as much air in the bag as you can (think unopened bag of chips) and cinch the top. Shake vigorously to coat the fries. Empty the bag into a mixing bowl and use your hands to toss with 1 tablespoon (15 ml) of the oil and half of the chipotle powder, if using. Arrange the fries on the prepared pan in a single layer, not touching. Repeat with the remaining fries, cornstarch, oil, and chipotle powder, if using.

Arrange the pans in the oven in the top and bottom thirds of the oven. Set the timer for 15 minutes. After 15 minutes, use a stiff spatula or fish turner to get under the fries and flip them over, again arranging in a single layer, not touching. Rotate the pans back to front and top to bottom and bake for an additional 10 to 15 minutes, or until they're brown and cooked through.

Shut off the oven, prop open the door halfway, and let them cool and crisp up further for 10 more minutes. Toss with salt to taste before serving.

NOTES:

Larger sweet potatoes are starchier, making them better texturally for fries. Go for the big ones!

You can use all cornstarch or a blend of corn starch, rice starch, potato starch, or tapioca starch. All will work well. I like a blend of cornstarch and brown rice starch.

Sweet Potatoes ANNA

There are few side dishes more visually appealing or simpler than Sweet Potatoes Anna; a cast-iron skillet full of thinly sliced sweet potatoes arranged in concentric circles, brushed with butter and sprinkled with fragrant thyme, and roasted to crisp edged, tender perfection. When it's turned out onto a plate, few things can compare to the beauty of this dish. Serve with roast pork, beef, chicken, or turkey and wait for the accolades!

YIELD: 8 SERVINGS

INGREDIENTS

¾ cup (170 g) butter

6 sprigs fresh thyme, divided, plus extra for garnish

3 lbs (1.4 kg) sweet potatoes, peeled and thinly sliced using a food processor or mandoline

1 tsp kosher salt, divided

1 tsp freshly ground black pepper, divided

Preheat the oven to 400°F (204°C). Place the butter in a 10-inch (25-cm) cast iron skillet with 2 sprigs of the thyme and place in the preheated oven just long enough to melt the butter. Use your fingers to strip the leaves off the rest of the thyme and set aside.

Remove the skillet, swirl to coat with the butter, and pour the butter into a heat-proof bowl.

In the same skillet, arrange the sweet potatoes in overlapping, concentric circles, brushing with the butter, sprinkling with ¼ teaspoon each of salt and pepper, and a quarter of the thyme leaves after each layer, until all of the potatoes are used up. This should yield about 4 layers.

Place a piece of foil, dull side against the potatoes, directly on the surface of the sweet potatoes. Place another heavy pan on top of the foil to compress the potato slices. If you don't have another oven-proof skillet, you can put an 8-inch (20-cm) round cake pan on top and weigh it down with a brick or two.

Bake for 45 minutes, or until the potatoes are easily pierced with a sharp knife. Run a thin metal spatula or a butter knife around the edge of the pan, place a plate on top of the skillet, and invert to remove the potato cake. Garnish with a few thyme leaves. Serve hot or warm in wedges.

WINTER SQUASH
(Butternut Squash, Kabocha, Etc....)

Winter squash is a marvel to me. It's usually tough to get into, hard to break down, and needs to be cooked to be edible, but boy is it worth it. The most commonly available varieties are the long, mellow gold butternut squash and the aptly named, green acorn squash which looks like a large version of its namesake. Giant kabocha squash are becoming more common, and any of those three types of squash can be used in these recipes.

My little sister, Christina, gets my eternal thanks and full credit for developing my favorite way to cook a squash; her genius method doesn't require wrestling a rolling squash while wielding a knife. It roasts the whole thing—kit and kaboodle—before you ever have to lift a knife. How to Roast a Whole Winter Squash Without Losing Your Fingers (page 238) is life changing, I tell you!

Squash Tots (page 241) enter the scene ready to help coax picky eaters into trying winter squash with an open mind. Sweet and savory, bite-size, and beautifully brown on the outside, these tots are so good that you might not want to share.

SHOPPING TIPS: Look for squash with no holes, soft spots, or cracks. The stem should be woody, hard, or corky, too. You want the squash to have a deep, saturated color (whichever variety you choose).

STORAGE: No refrigerator is necessary (or desirable) when it comes to storing these hardy squash. A 50°F (10°C) temperature in a dark, well-ventilated place is ideal and they can last in those conditions for 2 to 4 months.

HOW TO ROAST A WINTER SQUASH
Without Losing Your Fingers

My little sister, Christina, gets the credit for this brilliant slow-cooker recipe-slash-method for cooking winter squash that is my go-to in squash season. There's no need to wrestle a recalcitrant squash around the counter with a knife and pray you come out of it with all the fingers you had going into it as well as dinner. No knife is needed until the squash is fully cooked and ready to cooperate! Serve this roasted squash with roasted pork, chicken, or sausages. I love to serve a bowl full of the roasted squash topped with a generous pat of butter and glug of maple syrup.
Bonus: This makes a wonderful first food for babies!

YIELD: 4 SERVINGS PER SQUASH

INGREDIENTS

1–2 butternut, acorn, kabocha, calabaza, sugar pie pumpkin, or spaghetti squash (see Note)

Add your squash to the slow cooker. Cover with the lid and cook on LOW until the squash is easily pierced with a sharp knife at the thickest part of the squash; test at the neck for butternut squashes. The time this takes will depend largely on the size and type of squash you choose, but you can count on at least 4 hours for a smaller winter squash. Most squash that would fit into a slow cooker will be done in 8 hours of cooking time.

Use tongs or hot pads to carefully transfer the hot squash to a platter. Let it stand for 5 to 10 minutes, slice in half lengthwise, use a spoon to scoop out the seeds and strings, then scoop the flesh from the shells. If you're using spaghetti squash, use a fork to scrape the flesh out of the halved squash in the spaghetti like strands from one end to the other.

You can use the squash in this state or mashed and you can use it immediately or refrigerate or freeze it for later use.

For an incredibly festive side dish, run a potato masher through the roasted squash to break up any big chunks and transfer to an 8 x 8-inch (20 x 20-cm) baking dish. Dot the top with 6 tablespoons (85 g) of butter that has been cut into pats, and scatter ½ cup (110 g) of brown sugar over the top. Bake in a preheated 425°F (220°C) oven for 25 minutes, or until bubbly, then put under the broiler for about 3 minutes, or until there is a caramelized layer of molten sugar on top. Let rest for at least 5 minutes before serving directly from the pan.

NOTE

If you're cooking spaghetti squash, pierce it several times with a fork before adding the squash to the slow cooker.

SQUASH *Tots*

These savory and sweet, bite-size, crispy tots are a great way to introduce reluctant eaters to the joy that is winter squash. And if they won't eat it? Well, that's okay, because you're going to love them enough to eat them all by yourself!

YIELD: 4 SERVINGS

INGREDIENTS

1¼ cups (306 g) mashed roasted winter squash (page 238) (see Notes)

¼ cup (31 g) cornmeal

¼ cup (70 g) finely grated onion

1 tsp ground cumin

½ tsp chili powder

½ tsp smoked paprika

½ tsp kosher salt

Ketchup or Smoked Paprika Chipotle Sauce (page 252) for dipping

Preheat the oven to 350°F (176°C). Spray a half-sheet pan with nonstick cooking spray or brush lightly with oil. Set aside.

In a mixing bowl, vigorously stir the squash to be sure you have no chunks of squash. If needed, use a potato masher to break it up and smooth it out. Add in the cornmeal, onion, cumin, chili powder, paprika, and salt. Stir well to combine evenly.

Use a small cookie scoop to scoop the mixture into mounds on the prepared half-sheet pan, leaving a couple of inches of space between each one. Oil your hands and lightly press down to form a ¾-inch (2-cm) thick coin. Bake for 25 to 30 minutes, using a spatula to gently flip them over halfway through the cooking time, or until well browned and crisp on the outside. Transfer to a serving dish and serve with ketchup or Smoked Paprika Chipotle Sauce.

NOTES

This recipe works best with butternut, acorn, or kabocha squash.

If you do not have leftover roasted squash, you can start with 2 cups (232 g) of cubed squash, toss lightly with 1 teaspoon of olive oil, and roast on a rimmed sheet pan in a preheated 350°F (176°C) oven for 25 minutes, or until tender and golden brown at the edges. Mash the squash as directed above and proceed with the recipe.

SAVORY BUTTERNUT SQUASH *Soup*

Smooth and sublime, squash soup with a hint of sage is more than just a fun alliteration; it's a gorgeous, delicious, colorful, and simple side to a meal where the main is roast chicken, turkey, or pork. Leftovers freeze and reheat beautifully, so you can cook this autumnal and perfect meal starter and enjoy later, too. And handily, this stunning soup can be prepared in a slow cooker or on the stove top, whichever you prefer!

YIELD: 8 SERVINGS

INGREDIENTS

1 tbsp (15 ml) Luke's Infused Simon and Garfunkel Blend or Sage Oil (page 246) or regular olive oil

1 onion, peeled and diced

½ tsp kosher salt

4 cloves of garlic, peeled and minced

3 lbs (1.4 kg) butternut squash, peeled, halved, and cut into 2–3-inch (5–8-cm) chunks

1 apple, peeled, cored, and roughly chopped

1 carrot, peeled and roughly chopped

1 sprig fresh sage

3 cups (720 ml) vegetable or chicken stock

½ tsp ground black or white pepper

⅛ tsp cayenne pepper

⅛ tsp grated nutmeg

1 cup (240 ml) heavy cream, optional

¼ cup (35 g) pepitas, for garnish

½ tsp smoked paprika, for garnish

TO PREPARE ON THE STOVE TOP:

Heat the oil in a stockpot over medium heat. Add the onion and salt, tossing to coat. Sauté the onion for 5 minutes, stirring frequently. Add in the garlic and cook for 1 to 2 minutes, or until the garlic is fragrant. Add the squash, apple, carrot, sage, vegetable stock, black pepper, cayenne pepper, and nutmeg to the pot.

Bring the mixture to a simmer, cover tightly, and reduce the heat to medium-low. Simmer for 20 to 30 minutes, or until the squash is completely tender.

TO PREPARE IN A SLOW COOKER:

Heat the oil in a skillet over medium heat. Add the onion and salt, tossing to coat. Sauté the onion for 5 minutes, stirring frequently. Add in the garlic and cook for 1 to 2 minutes, or until the garlic is fragrant. Add the sautéed onion and garlic, squash, apple, carrot, sage, vegetable stock, black pepper, cayenne pepper, and nutmeg to the slow-cooker, cover with the lid, and cook on HIGH for 3 to 4 hours or LOW for 6 to 8 hours.

TO FINISH THE SOUP:

Remove and discard the sage. Use an immersion blender to puree the soup until completely smooth. Divide the soup between the serving bowls, swirl in 2 tablespoons (30 ml) of the heavy cream, if using, into each bowl, and garnish with pepitas and a sprinkle of smoked paprika shaken over the bowl with a fine mesh sieve.

NOTE

The heavy cream can be omitted if preferred, but it is a pretty addition!

Cheese Sauce OF CHAMPIONS

Every cook needs a great cheese sauce in their bag of tricks and thankfully, cheese sauce is super easy. Whether you're pouring this over roasted broccoli (page 32), dunking cauliflower tots (page 46), salt potatoes (page 17) or zucchini fries (page 78) in it, or drizzling onto one of the World's Best (and Easiest!) Baked Potatoes (page 21), this cheese sauce is going to be a mega hit at your house. This on boiled pasta is almost as fast as boxed macaroni and cheese and tastes far better! You can change up the cheese and spices you use to customize your cheese sauce, too!

YIELD: APPROXIMATELY 10 SERVINGS, OR 4 CUPS (960 ML)

. . . .

INGREDIENTS
3 tbsp (24 g) cornstarch

2½ cups (600 ml) milk, divided

½ tsp granulated onion

⅛ tsp finely ground pepper (preferably white)

2 cups (226 g) shredded sharp Cheddar cheese (see Notes)

¼ cup (25 g) freshly-grated Parmesan cheese

In a saucepan over medium-high heat, whisk together the cornstarch, ½ cup (120 ml) of the milk, granulated onion, and the pepper until smooth. Then drizzle in the rest of the milk slowly, whisking vigorously the whole time. Bring the mixture to a boil and boil for 2 minutes, whisking constantly.

Remove the pan from the heat and add the cheeses, using a spoon to stir until the cheeses are fully melted and incorporated. Store leftover cheese sauce tightly covered in the refrigerator. You can reheat the sauce gently in the microwave in 30 second bursts, stirring after each burst or in a saucepan over low heat.

NOTES
It is important that you take your sauce off the heat before adding the cheese, or it may become gritty.

For a slightly sharper sauce, add ½ teaspoon of dry mustard powder when you whisk in the granulated onion and pepper.

For a great nacho sauce, whisk in ½ teaspoon of ground cumin with the onion and pepper.

Swap out the Cheddar and Parmesan for 2¼ cups (252 g) of grated pepper Jack cheese for variety.

SMOKED PAPRIKA *Chipotle Sauce*

This visually pleasing and deliciously savory sauce has been a staple in our household for years and is destined to become one in your home, too. It goes on everything from burgers to sandwiches to rice bowls, is incorporated in many recipes as an ingredient, is a great sauce for all grilled meats and many roasted ones, too, and is a perfect reason to keep your pantry well stocked with chipotles in adobo sauce.

YIELD: APPROXIMATELY 10 SERVINGS, OR 2¼ CUPS (540 ML)

INGREDIENTS

1–3 chipotles in adobo, plus 1 tbsp (15 ml) of the adobo sauce (see Notes)

2 cloves of garlic, peeled and roughly chopped

Zest of 1 lemon

½ tsp kosher salt

2 cups (480 ml) mayonnaise

3 tbsp (21 g) smoked paprika

In a blender or food processor fitted with a metal blade, add the chipotles and adobo sauce with the garlic, lemon zest, and salt. Process until finely chopped. Add the mayonnaise and smoked paprika and blend, stopping to scrape down the sides of the machine at least once, until smooth and evenly colored. Please note that it is possible to over-process this and break the sauce, so go gently on it. Stop processing as soon as it is even in color.

Scrape into a jar or a squeeze bottle for easier delivery and refrigerate for up to 2 weeks.

NOTES

The sauce can be made as spicy as you'd like.

For an especially delicious Southwest-style salad dressing, whisk together ½ cup (120 ml) each of this Smoked Paprika Chipotle Sauce and Super Fresh Homemade Ranch Dressing (page 256).

GARLIC BUFFALO WING *Sauce*

I spend 6 days a week in Buffalo and consider myself something of an authority on Buffalo wings (which we actually refer to only as "wings") and wing sauce. In fact, I used to work in a pub where I whipped up thousands of chicken wings over the course of my employment. I'll leave it to Duff's and Anchor Bar to duke it out over who was first, but what everyone can agree on is that a great basic wing sauce is Frank's RedHot Sauce plus butter. I like to elevate wing sauce by gently roasting garlic cloves 'til tender in the butter we use for the sauce. This is the ne plus ultra of wing sauces, and you'll always want to keep a jar or two in your refrigerator for wings (obviously), our Buffalo-Roasted Potatoes (page 18), and our Buffalo Cauliflower "Wing" Bites (page 42). Let's go, Buffalo!

YIELD: APPROXIMATELY 16 SERVINGS, OR 3 CUPS (720 ML)

. . . .

INGREDIENTS

1 cup (227 g) unsalted butter, melted

10 cloves of garlic, peeled and lightly smacked to release the oils (You want to bruise the clove without smashing it.)

1⅓ cups (320 ml) hot sauce, I recommend Frank's RedHot (see Notes)

2 tbsp (30 ml) apple cider vinegar

2 tsp (10 ml) Worcestershire

¼ tsp ground cayenne pepper

In a small saucepan, melt the butter with the garlic cloves over low heat. Let the mixture bubble gently until the garlic cloves become tender, about 10 minutes. Take care not to "toast" the butter or garlic cloves, removing from the heat as needed to prevent browning. Add the hot sauce, vinegar, Worcestershire, and cayenne, whisk it together, and bring the sauce to a boil over medium-high heat. Boil for 2 minutes, whisking constantly. Remove the sauce from the heat and allow it to cool for 5 minutes before blending until smooth with a stick blender or a regular blender. Transfer the sauce to a jar to refrigerate. Store for up to 1 month. It may separate as it cools, so whisk it together before using.

NOTES

For mild Garlic Buffalo Wing Sauce, change the quantity of butter to 1⅔ cups (377 g) and the Frank's RedHot Sauce to ⅔ cup (160 ml).

For medium Garlic Buffalo Wing Sauce, change the quantity of butter to 1⅓ cups (302 g) and the Frank's RedHot Sauce to 1 cup (240 ml).

For extra spicy Garlic Buffalo Wing Sauce, change the quantity of butter to ⅔ cup (150 g) and the Frank's RedHot Sauce to 1⅔ cups (400 ml).

BETTER-THAN-STORE-BOUGHT
Ranch Dressing TWO WAYS

Everyone loves ranch dressing and for good reason; it's creamy, it's full of herbs, and it makes everything it touches more appealing. While you can buy packets of dry mix to make your own ranch at home, it's just as easy (and arguably better for you) to whip up your own.

FOR HOMEMADE RANCH DRESSING MIX

⅓ cup (28 g) dry buttermilk powder (see Notes)

3 tbsp (5 g) dried parsley flakes, divided

2½ tsp (6 g) granulated garlic

2½ tsp (5 g) granulated onion

2 tsp (2 g) dried dill weed

2 tsp (2 g) dried onion flakes

2 tsp (1 g) dried chives

1½ tsp (9 g) kosher salt

1 tsp coarsely ground black pepper

FOR SUPER FRESH HOMEMADE RANCH DRESSING

1¼ cups (300 ml) cultured buttermilk (see Notes)

1 cup (240 ml) sour cream

¾ cup (180 ml) mayonnaise

⅓ cup packed (15 g) finely chopped fresh dill weed

¼ cup packed (15 g) finely chopped fresh parsley

¼ cup (12 g) finely chopped chives or green parts only of green onions

¾ tsp finely chopped fresh oregano leaves

1–2 large cloves of garlic, peeled and finely minced or pressed with a garlic press

1 tsp kosher salt

½ tsp coarsely ground black pepper

FOR HOMEMADE RANCH DRESSING MIX

Put the buttermilk powder, 1½ tablespoons (2.5 g) of the parsley flakes, granulated garlic and onion, dill weed, onion flakes, chives, salt, and pepper in the carafe of a blender. Pulse about 8 to 15 times, or until the onion flakes, parsley, and chives are broken down very small and almost powdered like commercially available ranch dressing mix. Stir in the remaining parsley flakes and transfer to a jar with a tight-fitting lid. Store the mix in a tightly lidded container at cool room temperature in a dark place for up to 6 months. You may need to break up clumps from time to time. Shake the closed container to do so, or use a fork to break apart especially tenacious clumps.

TO MAKE RANCH DRESSING FROM YOUR MIX

Whisk together 1 cup (240 ml) of milk, 1 cup (240 ml) of mayonnaise, and 3 tablespoons (45 g) of your dry mix until smooth. Refrigerate for 30 minutes before serving. Use the prepared dressing within a week.

TO MAKE SUPER FRESH HOMEMADE RANCH DRESSING

Whisk together the buttermilk, sour cream, mayonnaise, dill weed, parsley, chives, oregano, garlic, salt, and pepper, until smooth. Pour into a jar or squeeze bottle and refrigerate for 30 minutes before serving. This dressing will keep well in the refrigerator for up to a week.

NOTES

Buttermilk powder can be purchased through many online retailers including Amazon, King Arthur Flour, and Walmart.

This dressing is at its best flavor and texture-wise when made with cultured buttermilk. If you can't find cultured buttermilk, you can substitute 1 cup (240 ml) of plain yogurt (not Greek). If you don't have yogurt handy, you can add 1 tablespoon (15 ml) of white vinegar to a measuring cup and then add enough milk to make 1 cup (240 ml). Let it stand at room temperature for 5 minutes. It won't be quite as smooth a finished dressing as it would be if you used buttermilk or yogurt, but it will taste good.

Let Me Break It Down for You!:

HELPFUL TECHNIQUES FOR BREAKING DOWN OR CUTTING VARIOUS VEGETABLES

One thing to remember in cutting and breaking down vegetables is that the goal is to minimize the amount of moving around that vegetables do while you're working on them. Some of those round little beasties have a distressing tendency to roll around on the cutting board and that just isn't safe.

The most important and universal rule of all is to keep your knives sharp! A sharp knife is a safe knife, and makes quick work of breaking down vegetables. You don't have to work as hard to cut with them and that in and of itself is a safety feature. The harder you have to push on a knife, the more likely it is to slip in an unpleasant way. Additionally, should you accidentally nick yourself with a sharp knife, your cut will be a much cleaner-edged, tidier cut that will heal much more easily than a jagged cut from a dull knife.

Bonus: A sharp knife also diminishes the tears you may experience while cutting onions. When you cut an onion, you're breaking cell walls and releasing volatile sulfur compounds which are the meanies responsible for making you tear up. A sharper knife cuts more cleanly than a dull knife which rips, meaning fewer cell walls are damaged and less sulfur is released. Voila! Tear free (or nearly, anyway) onion cutting!

HOW TO DICE ONIONS

This one is a doozy for many people and the correct method for dicing an onion is a revelation if you've never learned it. Your life will be easier from here on in if this is your first time hearing it.

1. Cut a disc from the blossom end of the onion so the onion can stand steady on the cutting board without rolling away. Place the onion on that cut surface.

2. Cut downward through the hairy root end of the onion, dividing the onion in half. Peel the peel backward over the roots, leaving it intact like a handle.

3. Holding your knife parallel to your cutting board, make one cut from the middle of the front of the onion toward the root end, without cutting through the root.

4. Moving your knife above the onion and holding it perpendicular to the root, make several parallel slices downward with the knife tip ¼-inch (6-mm) from the root. Another way to think of this is to cut several parallel slices from the north pole (root end) of the onion to the south pole (where the blossom end was) through to the cutting board. The number of cuts you make will determine the size of your dice.

5. Turn the onion and slice downward across those cuts for perfectly diced onions.

HOW TO CUT FLORETS FROM CAULIFLOWER AND BROCCOLI

Mercifully, cauliflower and broccoli provide their own little roadmaps to perfect florets, but there is a time saving technique you can employ.

With broccoli, cut the stem away from the crown of broccoli as close to the crown as you can. Preserve that broccoli stem! (See pages 36 and 39 for delicious salads to make with them.)

1. Cut the head of cauliflower or crown of broccoli in half from top to bottom through the core and then into quarters. Lay the quarters cut side down on the cutting board.

2. Slide your knife in and cut between the florets and the stem. The cauliflower or broccoli will now fall into large florets.

3. You can use your fingers or your knife to break the large florets into bite sized ones.

HOW TO BREAK DOWN A GREEN OR RED CABBAGE

A dense, perfectly round head of cabbage can be a little intimidating and seems a bit like a bowling ball under a knife. Never fear, though, here's the break down on breaking it down.

1. Remove the outermost leaves of the cabbage.

2. Most heads of cabbage have a relatively flat stem. Perch the cabbage on it and cut downward from the north pole to the south pole of the cabbage.

3. Lay the cabbage halves, cut side down, on the cutting board and cut in half again from pole to pole. This should expose the core of the cabbage.

4. Cut the core out of the cabbage quarters.

5. To make bite-size pieces, make two or three cuts lengthwise down the cabbage quarter, then turn and cut across those to create bite-size pieces.

6. To shred the cabbage for coleslaw, turn the cabbage quarters perpendicular to your knife and slice thinly across the quarters.

THE MOST CONVENIENT WAY TO BREAK DOWN BELL PEPPERS

1. Hold the pepper upright by the stem with the base on the cutting board.

2. Make four downward cuts around the outside edge from top to bottom of the pepper. This should remove the flesh and leave the seeds and stem in the center.

3. You can now cut the slabs lengthwise into strips of desired width.

4. If you'd like diced peppers, cut across the strips to create diced peppers.

HOW TO REMOVE CORN KERNELS FROM THE COB

1. Place the bottom of the shucked ear of corn onto the bottom side of a paper plate on a large cutting board (or in a large mixing bowl, if you prefer to contain the kernels) while holding the top of the ear with your hand.

2. Slide the knife down from pole to pole separating the kernels from the cob.

Resources

. . . .

VEGETABLE SUBSCRIPTION BOXES BY REGION (UNITED STATES ONLY)

Below you'll find three of the biggest, most well-known produce subscription services. There are many more that exist to serve much smaller geographical areas. If you'd like to look for a locally-run operation, please search for the phrase "vegetable subscription box [your zip code]" on an internet search engine. Even Amazon offers a few heartier vegetable boxes!

MISFITS MARKET

This is a service and company that I use regularly. They offer boxes full of "imperfect but delicious" produce at a savings of 25% to 40% less than the equivalent produce would cost at a grocery store. They also offer a referral program so if you love it and tell your friends, you'll both get a discount.

As of writing, these are available in Alabama, Connecticut, Delaware, Florida, Georgia, Illinois, Indiana, Kentucky, Maine, Maryland, Massachusetts, New Hampshire, New Jersey, New York, North Carolina, Ohio, Pennsylvania, Rhode Island, South Carolina, Tennessee, Vermont, Virginia, Washington, D.C., and West Virginia, with plans to expand into more markets.

www.misfitsmarket.com

FARMBOX DIRECT

Their website states they deliver to everywhere in the Continental United States and offers a selection between all natural, all organic, all fruits, all vegetables, or a combination of all of them in small-, medium-, and large-sized boxes. They also offer specialized juicing boxes. Farmbox Direct also offers a loyalty/referral program.

www.farmboxdirect.com

HUNGRY HARVEST

Hungry Harvest is another service that helps "rescue" cosmetically imperfect, but perfectly edible produce and delivers to Maryland, Washington, D.C., Virginia, Greater Philadelphia, Southern New Jersey, Northern Delaware, South Florida, The Triangle Area & Charlotte in North Carolina & the Detroit Metro Area. They also offer a waitlist because they're expanding into more delivery areas.

https://www.hungryharvest.net

SPICES, VINEGAR, AND MORE

If your local stores don't carry some of the ingredients called for in this book—I'm looking at you gochugaru and doenjang—you can easily order them online through Amazon.com, iGourmet.com, WorldMarket.com, thrivemarket.com, spicejungle.com, and many, many more online retailers. The internet is our friend here.

COMMUNITY SUPPORTED AGRICULTURE (C.S.A)

The best way to find a local CSA is to ask your friends! I was shocked when I learned how many CSA organizations existed in my own rural area. If your friends haven't heard of it, don't worry: we have the internet to help us! Search for "CSA [your zip code]" using an internet search engine and be prepared to be wowed.

Acknowledgments

· ·

To all of my Foodie with Family readers: THANK YOU! Your kind words and questions over the years have kept me motivated to create more delicious recipes to share. I am so grateful for each and every one of you and cherish the comments and emails I get from you.

To my husband, Lindy: as always, your name goes on this book because there's no one I'd rather do life with than you. I love you. Plus, you're super handsome.

To my boys, Liam, Aidan, Ty, Leif, and Rowan: Thanks for forcing me to get creative with vegetables over the years and thanks for being adventurous enough to learn with me. I love you guys bigger than the bay and am incredibly proud of what you're doing with your lives.

To my *Goûteuse Officielle et belle-fille*, Anaïs: thank you for being my first "daughter". I'm grateful for your wit, charm, kindness, and endless willingness to try all vegetable dishes—most especially the beet dishes—that I make. Best first daughter-in-law, EVER!

To my Mom and Dad, Jess, Nate, Luke, Christina, Airlia, Christi, Lynne, Mary, Meseidy, Ali, Bronwen, Heidi, Leela, Kim, Michelle, Maggie (for the squash soup idea!) Sergio, my editor Marissa Giambelluca and the whole team at Page Street Publishing, thank you for your support and for tasting everything and bouncing ideas with me! To my boys' friends Austin Propert, Joel and Christopher Danner, and Booker Liddick thank you for being taste testers!

And, as always, my biggest thanks are reserved for God: "Taste and see that the Lord is good, blessed is the one who takes refuge in Him." Psalm 34:8

About the Author

· ·

REBECCA LINDAMOOD is bringing her love for all vegetables to the dinner table with her third cookbook. A long-time vegetable lover, she knew she'd met her soulmate when her husband ordered his meal with a request to "run it through the garden" on one of their first dates.

She is the creator of the Foodie with Family website and the two-time cookbook author of *Not Your Mama's Canning Book: Modern Canned Goods and What to Make with Them* as well as *Ready, Set, Dough!: Beginner Breads for All Occasions*.

In addition to full-time food blogging, she is a part-time ballet and movement photographer. She is crazy about the Oxford comma, all kinds of tea, pizza, pudding, and her ridiculous menagerie of critters.

She lives in Western New York where she is married to her biggest culinary fan. Together they have raised five wild, crazy, charming, talented boys and been gifted one fabulous daughter-in-law.

Index